Caernarfon Castle, birthplace of Edward II and scene of two investiture ceremonies. Photo © Rhys Jones, LRPS.

A POCKET GUIDE

PRINCES OF WALES

DEBORAH FISHER

UNIVERSITY OF WALES PRESS
CARDIFF
2006

British Library Cataloguing in Publication Data
A catalogue record for this book is available from the British Library

ISBN-10 0-7083-2003-1
ISBN-13 978-07083-2003-7

Printed in Great Britain by Antony Rowe Ltd, Wiltshire

Contents

The Story of the First Prince of Wales

One day in 1284, King Edward I was sitting in his quarters at Caernarfon Castle, looking fondly on as his wife played with their new-born son, when he became aware of a commotion outside.

'What's all that noise?' he asked a courtier.

'It's the Welsh, sir,' came the reply. 'They are complaining about how you killed their prince and forced them to live under English rule.'

'I see,' said the king, striding up to the battlements. 'We'll soon put a stop to that.'

When the people observed that their efforts had resulted in King Edward coming out personally to have a look at what was going on, they went suddenly quiet.

'I understand you are not happy to be ruled by an English king,' he shouted.

A few of the crowd (those who understood English) responded bravely, and others, seeing that they got away with it, followed the lead.

'Perhaps you would prefer a prince of your own,' Edward continued.

There was a murmur of approval, tempered with suspicion, as the word passed among the crowd and was translated.

'If I give you a prince, one born in Wales, who speaks not a word of English, will you accept him and stop making a fuss?'

This was too good to be true. The crowd responded with a big cheer.

Edward went back into the castle, and emerged a few moments later, carrying his own baby son.

'Here he is!' he cried. 'The new Prince of Wales! Now shut up and go home.'

It's a good story. Unfortunately, there is no historical evidence that it ever happened.

Introduction

One phenomenon encountered when considering the significance of the title 'Prince of Wales' is that there will not always be someone to hold it. If, for example, Prince William were to ascend the throne immediately after his grandmother (and there are several possible events that might result in this scenario), he may never hold the title of Prince of Wales himself. If he comes to the throne before having children of his own, there will be no Prince of Wales until a son is born. If he has only daughters, there will be no Prince of Wales until the next monarch succeeds. If that monarch has no sons, the cycle will be repeated. The world being as it is in the twenty-first century, it is highly likely that the next few monarchs will come to the throne as adults, but there is no guarantee that they will already be, or will ever become, parents.

Furthermore, there is the question of equal rights for women. Some countries have already altered their laws of succession so that sons no longer take precedence over daughters. European legislation on human rights demands such a development. Since a woman cannot, by definition, be Prince of Wales, some other title may need to be found in the future; 'Princess of Wales' is not an option, since that title is reserved for the *wife* of a Prince of Wales. We cannot foresee how long the concept of Prince of Wales, in its present form, will last, nor can we predict whether there will always be a connection between the principality of Wales and the reigning monarch. This book can only look back on history and review how things have been done in the past.

The main difference between this and my previous book, *Princesses of Wales*, is that there have been fewer than half as many princesses as there have been princes. For this reason, there is less space for individual biographical detail about the holders of the title. The lives of some of these men (and boys) have been subject to much previous commentary and analysis. *Princes of Wales* aims to give roughly equal space to all the princes, whilst taking into account the relative lengths of their lives and their political significance. In other words, a prince who went on to become king, won or lost battles and passed major legislation will get more attention than a prince who died at the age of ten. Nevertheless, the prince who died aged ten will receive as much attention in this book as is allowed by the known facts of his life.

There is little room to explore the history of the medieval princes of Wales. This has been done more thoroughly by academic historians of the calibre of the late Professor R. R. Davies, and it would be a departure from this book's true subject to attempt to recreate this research. The activities of those pre-conquest princes are discussed only when directly relevant.

Any attempt to identify the first Prince of Wales is doomed to failure. The difficulty lies not only in the definition of 'prince' but also in the definition of 'Wales'. The country we know today came into existence mainly because the western Celts became separated from the northern Celts by the Saxon invasion. This was a lengthy and imprecise procedure that eventually resulted in a distinct geographical area, with a people who spoke a common language, separated by a natural border from others who did not. The subsequent Norman conquest was carried out piecemeal, with the southerners of Morgannwg and Gwent the first to be picked off. The final victory was a bloody and dramatic one, and it is this that makes Llywelyn the Last many people's choice as the last 'true' Prince of Wales. In fact, he was one of the *first* to hold the title. For most of the Middle Ages (defined as the period between the Roman abandonment of Britain and the coming of the Tudors), Wales consisted of a multitude of territories, some quite tiny, each of which had its own ruler. The term 'prince' and its Welsh equivalent, 'tywysog', only came into common usage towards the end of that period.

The difference between a prince and a king tends to be popularly recognized in terms of total area ruled; thus there is a king of Spain, but not a king of Luxembourg. On the other hand, a little country like Swaziland or Bhutan may have a 'king'. Wales had its kings, rulers who brought most if not all of the country under their sway. The factor that made the later medieval Welsh princes something lower than kings was that, despite being absolute rulers on a day-to-day basis, they were officially subservient to their neighbours, the kings of England. In order to avoid conflict, the Norman rulers agreed to keep out of Wales if the Welsh rulers acknowledged Norman supremacy. From the mid eleventh century until the late thirteenth, the Welsh paid lip service to this requirement. The final showdown was brought about by a personal feud between two very stubborn men who both happened to be excellent warriors, and it ended, inevitably, in the humiliation and subjugation of the smaller country.

When, in 1969, the present Prince of Wales was invested with the title at Caernarfon Castle, he swore an oath to 'bear faith and truth' to his monarch 'to live and die against all manner of folks'. The recipient of the oath, whose 'liege man of life and limb' Charles claimed to be, was none other than his mother. This apparently insignificant fact is the key to the difference between the 'Welsh' princes of Wales and their 'English' successors. When a medieval prince was forced to pay homage to a greater prince (in other words, a king) for his possessions, there was not normally a close family relationship involved. Following the Norman invasion of England, the new dynasty considered that they owned Wales, even though they had not yet conquered it. Before the arrival of William I, Saxon kings were claiming precedence over the native rulers, though somewhat less confidently than became the case after the Norman victory at the Battle of Hastings.

On occasions, it suited the Welsh princes to accept this arrangement, where they were nominally subservient to an English overlord, in return for the benefits the feudal system offered them, namely protection. In paying homage to King Henry II of England, Owain Gwynedd knew that he could, theoretically, call on Henry to support him in the case of a military conflict with any of his near neighbours, something that was generally more likely than a war with the English. One or two Norman kings of England were obliged to breach the borders of Wales in order to ensure that the Welsh understood that they had the power to enforce their superiority if the occasion called for it; but they did not always come off best. Until the reign of King John, no one pressed the point. John was proactive; he saw the advantage of an alliance with the Welsh, perhaps noting how many Norman nobles had acquired a foothold by marriage into the local nobility. Accordingly, he married off his illegitimate daughter, Joan, to Llywelyn ap Iorwerth, whom we know better as Llywelyn Fawr or 'Llywelyn the Great', one of very few Welsh rulers who had both military ability and political acumen. Llywelyn was a realist and an opportunist; even so, he was often at odds with his father-in-law. An exceptional man, he almost succeeded in uniting Wales under a single ruler, but he had to compromise to achieve as much as he did.

Under John's successor, the weak but long-lived Henry III, Anglo-Welsh relations improved somewhat, and the Welsh began to take advantage of the family ties. Llywelyn Fawr was granted the title Prince of North Wales by his brother-in-law. His legitimate son by Joan, Dafydd ap Llywelyn, was the first to be officially recognized by the English as 'Prince of Wales', though he still had to pay homage to the English king in order to be sure of the title. In 1247, after Dafydd's death, the Treaty of Woodstock gave away certain Welsh possessions to King Henry, and in 1254 all the Crown lands in Wales were placed in the charge of Henry's son, Prince Edward. This was a hint as to what would follow when Edward reached maturity and succeeded his father as King Edward I.

Things might have worked out very differently had Dafydd been a more worthy successor to his father, had he not been childless, and had he not died in his thirties. It was left to Dafydd's nephew, Llywelyn ap Gruffydd, to attempt to restore the fortunes of the principality of Gwynedd, which he ruled, and that of Wales, which he aspired to rule. He is known as 'Llywelyn the Last', which just about sums up his career. In 1265, Llywelyn was separately recognized as Prince of Wales and ruler of the principality. By the 1267 Treaty of Montgomery, King Henry III granted to Llywelyn and his heirs the right to be styled Prince of Wales and to possess the lands that went with it. This did *not* include the lands that already belonged to the Normans.

The terms of the treaty lasted for less than twenty years. Llywelyn ap Gruffydd was a noble but flawed character, who aroused antagonism where none was needed. Perhaps his biggest disadvantage came in the form of three brothers, all with less ability than his but with equal ambition. Thus it was that Edward I was presented with both the opportunity and the excuse to invade Wales. Another stroke of bad luck brought Llywelyn's life to an end, and the obvious successor, his brother Dafydd ap Gruffydd, lacked both the charisma and the determination to gather the support needed in order to continue the struggle.

Edward I, now in effective possession of the whole of Wales, saw the need for reconciliation. The story of the making of the 'first' Prince of Wales at Caernarfon is apocryphal; but there is no doubt that Edward did create his eldest surviving son Prince of Wales in 1301. Such an arrangement was not unprecedented. It was, however, a new departure for this corner of Europe, to give a son such a substantial possession and income, whilst forcing him to pay homage to his father for it. The rest is history.

Some Interesting Statistics

Buckingham Palace recognizes twenty-one 'official' Princes of Wales since 1301. This excludes: Edward III, Henry VI and Edward VI (who, though heirs apparent, were never officially given the title), and 'Bonnie Prince Charlie', who claimed it unofficially. It also excludes Owain Glyndŵr, who was recognized as Prince of Wales by some foreign governments, but never by the English. Two of the official princes (Edward II and Henry V) were actually born in Wales, as was Owain Glyndŵr. Of the other official princes, two were born in Scotland, two in Germany, one in France, and the remainder in England. (Bonnie Prince Charlie was born in Italy.)

Of the twenty-one princes, only thirteen have gone on to become king. They were: Edward II, Richard II, Henry V, Edward V (briefly), Henry VIII, Charles I, Charles II, George II, George III, George IV, Edward VII, George V and Edward VIII (again briefly). Edward II, Henry VIII, Charles I and George V all came into the title as the result of the death of an older brother, and both Richard II and George III obtained it because of the premature deaths of their fathers. These last two were the only holders of the title not to be sons of a monarch.

Only one Prince of Wales has died in battle: Edward of Westminster, the son of King Henry VI. Edward of Middleham, Arthur Tudor and Henry Stuart all died before coming of age; the Black Prince and Frederick, Prince of Wales, died as adults, as did James Stuart, the 'Old Pretender', who claimed but never regained his father's throne. The average age of Princes of Wales at the time of their death (not counting the present prince) is 47, and their average age at time of first marriage is 25.

Between them, the twenty-one official princes produced a total of 102 living children in the course of their lives, impressive when you bear in mind that seven of them never had any children at all. Twenty-nine of the above-mentioned children were illegitimate, with the most bastards having been produced by Charles II – who left no legitimate heir. Of the legitimate children, only thirty were born to men who were Prince of Wales at the time (the others were born when their fathers held different titles). Nineteen of these were boys and only eleven were girls. The children of a Prince of Wales are styled 'Prince(ss) of Wales'. They retain this style until either their father comes to the throne or they are given another title.

Only eleven of the official princes are known for certain to have visited the principality in their lifetimes: Edward II, Richard II, Henry V, Edward of Westminster, Charles I, Charles II, George IV, Edward VII, George V, Edward VIII and Charles, the present prince. Several other princes were either resident in Ludlow or spent time in the Marches, and may have ventured over the border without any record having been kept of the occasion: these were Edward, the Black Prince, Edward V, Arthur Tudor and Henry VIII.

Since 1301, the title of Prince of Wales has been vacant for approximately half its existence. The longest gap was that of 101 years between the accession to the throne of Henry VIII on 21 April 1509, and the investiture of Henry Stuart on 4 June 1610. The most enduring of the princes was Edward VII, who held the title from 1841 right up to his accession in 1901 – a total of nearly sixty years. He is closely followed by George IV, who held it from 1762 up to his accession in 1820. The present Prince of Wales has used the title since 1958, making him third in the longevity stakes. There is a strong possibility that he will outlast them all.

Edward of Caernarfon, the first 'official' Prince of Wales.
From a Victorian print.

The Conquest of Edward I
and Creation of the Principality

King Edward I of England saw a need for complete domination of Wales, as none of his predecessors had done. His name is reviled in histories of the Welsh and Scottish peoples, but more for his apparent ruthlessness and brutality than for his ability as a monarch, which was, clearly, considerable. Had Llywelyn ap Gruffydd and his brothers been of similar calibre, today's map of the UK might look very different.

Edward's motivation appears to have been part personal and part political. He and Llywelyn came to hate one another, largely because Llywelyn insisted on allying himself with the de Montfort family, Edward's cousins and sworn enemies. The more Edward asserted himself, the more Llywelyn kicked against the traces. The more Llywelyn indulged in petty gestures, the more harshly Edward struck back. The final military conflict was not inevitable, but it ended with most of south Wales (already well integrated with Norman rule) under Edward's proverbial thumb, and the remaining north Walean opposition reduced to nothing.

Looking back on these events from a distance of 700 years makes us inclined to see them in a false light. It may fairly be said that, though the concept of *nationality* may have existed for the Welsh, the concept of *nationhood* did not. The people of Wales recognized themselves as the remnant of the ancient British people, bound together by language, traditions and geography. They did not see their country as a single nation-state, and few men had ever attempted to rule, let alone succeeded in ruling, the whole of Wales. Indeed, the tribes prided themselves on their independence of one another. Llywelyn's attempt to fulfil his grandfather's vision of a united Wales, able to resist Norman incursions, was destined to fail, not because of the military dominance of the English, but because of opposition from his fellow Welshmen. One might draw a parallel with the Wales of today, where a majority of the population takes pleasure in decrying the efforts of the few who sit in the Assembly, partly because they recognize them as their equals and not their superiors.

In 1284, the Statute of Rhuddlan made Wales a part of England. In his own words, Edward I:

> wholly and entirely transferred under our proper dominion, the land of Wales, with its inhabitants, heretofore subject unto us, in feudal right, all obstacles whatsoever ceasing; and hath annexed and united the same unto the crown of the aforesaid realm, as a member of the same body.

New counties were created, including Caernarvonshire, Anglesey, Merionethshire, Cardiganshire and Carmarthenshire, all modelled on the existing administrative structure of England. The power of the Marcher lords was left more or less intact; Edward owed them a big favour for helping to distract Llywelyn in the last years of his rule.

Edward built his famous string of castles across the country, of which the jewel in the crown was Caernarfon, but it was pure chance that resulted in his son, the future Edward II, being born there. The young prince was neither his father's first son nor his heir, and the idea of making him Prince of Wales may have come later, out of the memory of his birth linked with the recognition that the Welsh were not going to submit to English rule without resentment. Was it this that led Edward I, in 1301, to invest his son with the title?

The fifteenth-century chronicler Thomas Walsingham claims that the Welsh people welcomed their new prince heartily, considering him one of them, thanks to his place of birth. It is extremely doubtful whether this is true. It is probably true, however, that a section of the population, those who had prospered under Norman rule, welcomed his appointment to the title. In many ways, it was a good sign. No more the emphasis on French titles for the son of the English king. Edward I had decided that the future of his dynasty lay within the British Isles.

What the title actually meant, at the time, is unclear. Although the tradition of naming the heir apparent Prince of Wales has continued up to the present day, its adoption was not immediate.

When Edward II in turn had a son of his own, he did not create him Prince of Wales, and there were many subsequent monarchs of England who hesitated before bestowing the title on their heirs. Some seem to have regarded it as tempting fate, giving the heir to the throne a personal power base from which, potentially, to rebel against his father, something not hitherto unknown amongst Norman rulers. Only gradually did it come to be regarded as a birthright.

That, however, was all in the future on 7 February 1301, when Edward II, aged sixteen, attended an investiture ceremony at a parliament in Lincoln. Parliament would be the normal venue for such events for most of the title's history. In the period since Edward's birth at Caernarfon, his elder brother Alfonso had died, leaving him the heir to the throne. Along with the title, Edward acquired the revenues of the principality of Wales. Apart from that, it is not clear whether the land of his birth meant anything to him. One thing that is certain, however, is that every one of the 'English' Princes of Wales who followed him, apart from the Black Prince, had the blood of Llywelyn Fawr in his veins. This is perhaps the greatest of the many ironies we will encounter as we journey through the history of the title.

What were these mysterious 'revenues' payable to the Prince of Wales? And what happens to them when there is no prince? In the time of Edward I, it was straightforward enough. Any taxes and rents paid by the people of Wales to the English Crown became the property of the Prince of Wales. When there was no prince, they belonged to the King of England.

Things changed gradually, with the shift towards parliamentary government culminating in a constitutional monarchy where Parliament decided how much pocket money the royal family ought to have. In the present day, the Prince of Wales administers property worth millions of pounds, and most of this has nothing to do with Wales. His traditional second title, Duke of Cornwall, is far more profitable, entailing, as it does, the ownership of vast estates. Readers may already be asking the question, 'What happens when there is no Duke of Cornwall?' The answer is much the same as for the Prince of Wales's revenues.

The principality as it stood at the beginning of the fourteenth century did not include the whole of what we now know as Wales. Certain lordships and counties were granted to other nobles, including Roger Mortimer, Earl of March, who would later have a significant role to play in the history of the English monarchy. March was not a place, but a region, the 'marches' of Wales.

The granting of all Crown lands to Edward, the first Prince of Wales, was not without precedent. In 1254, his grandfather, Henry III, had invested the heir to the throne, Edward I himself, with the Welsh possessions of the English Crown, as well as certain other royal possessions, including the county or 'palatinate' of Chester. This event demonstrates that the creation of the principality was not as sudden or dramatic as we have been taught, but was a natural development. Those who swore an oath of allegiance to their new overlord included both English and Welsh nobles, and for many of them it made little difference whether they swore it direct to the king or to his eldest son. Moreover, it was written into the terms of the investiture that the lands given by the king to his heir would remain the prince's possession when he in turn became king. It was this that made the principality a permanent entity which would survive regardless of who held the throne.

It is worth emphasizing that the Prince of Wales does not and did not *own* Wales, nor did he ever rule it except in the most honorary way. The title provided a focus for the interests of the Welsh landowners and their tenants, but only in the Middle Ages (i.e. before the Acts of Union) was this of great significance. By the time of the Hanoverians, even the entitlement to the revenues of the principality had ceased to be automatic, and during the eighteenth century Parliament stopped granting them to the Prince of Wales.

Edward of Caernarfon, the first 'English' Prince of Wales, is one of those whose record as prince is least easy to assess. His role was not fixed; his father resembled those managers who tell under-occupied minions that 'the job is what you make of it'. A council of fifteen was appointed to help the prince run the country. The Justices of north and south Wales were his seconds-in-command, and he was apparently not expected to take an active role in the government of his principality, which was not of course subject to the same laws as England. Whatever the younger Edward did, 'Longshanks' was almost guaranteed to be dissatisfied with it. His own record of conquest was so impressive that his son could never have lived up to it, even if there had been some material incentive. The incentive would come only after Edward I's death. In the meantime, the king's barons did not care for the elevation of the heir apparent to a title such as Prince of Wales.

The son followed the father's lead in all matters of importance. Edward of Caernarfon served with distinction in the king's Scottish campaign, and showed little fear of the northern menace during the last days of William Wallace's resistance. By the time he turned twenty-one, he had 200 courtiers of his own, but he spent the majority of his time hunting, hawking and jousting. He was knighted at Westminster, along with his great friend, Piers Gaveston, a Gascon nobleman. The plan was that he would lead the next Scottish campaign. The king was already in poor health; on his way to support his son, he died near Carlisle.

Edward II succeeded to the throne in 1307. During his reign, Welsh members were first summoned to the English Parliament, forty-eight of them in all. Welshmen joined the King of England's army, and would make a significant contribution to the success of that army in the course of the Hundred Years War. Under Edward II, the regime in Wales would not be as oppressive as it had been in the years immediately following his father's conquest. There was, after all, no single native leader with the power to represent a real threat to his supremacy. Hundreds of the prince's tenants had sworn an oath of fealty; most did so in writing, but the more prominent among them did so in person. Edward had little to fear from his Welsh subjects. It was from his fellow Englishmen that the opposition would come.

Popular history has it that Edward of Caernarfon was homosexual. This is far from being proven; but it is certain that he was under the influence of successive male favourites, beginning with Piers Gaveston, whose arrogance made him no friends. Gaveston having been the cause of a barons' rebellion which ended with his permanent removal from the scene in 1312, Edward demonstrated his inability to learn from his mistakes by taking a new favourite, Hugh le Despenser, who eventually met with the same fate at the hands of the disgruntled opposition.

Shortly after taking the throne, Edward married Isabella, daughter of Philippe IV of France. They had four healthy children, demonstrating that Edward, even if his preferences lay elsewhere, was well able to fulfil his marital obligations. By all accounts, he was a fine figure of a man, strong and athletic. In the end, this was the reason it took him so long to die.

As a king he was an abject failure. He lost the hold his father had gained on Scotland, suffering an embarrassing defeat at Bannockburn in 1314 at the hands of the opportunist Robert Bruce. He allowed the government of England to be dominated by his personal favourites, to the annoyance of most of the nobility. In 1322, he rescinded the ordinances imposed on him by the barons earlier in his reign, and at the Battle of Boroughbridge he fought his own cousin, Thomas, Earl of Lancaster, a man who had previously been one of the king's most loyal supporters. After a show trial presided over by the king's favourite, Hugh le Despenser, and the latter's father, the Earl of Winchester, Lancaster was executed. Like Gaveston before them, the Despensers had been recalled from exile by the king.

It was Despenser the younger who made enemies in Wales by the execution of Llywelyn Bren in 1316. A south Wales noble-man, Bren had dared to stand up for the rights of the local popu-lation when they were afflicted with heavy taxes. He surrendered on the understanding that his followers would be spared. The king promised him a pardon. Both promises were broken.

Fatally, Edward alienated his wife, Isabella, the 'She-Wolf of France'. The queen promptly took up with the Marcher lord, Roger Mortimer (a descendant of Llywelyn Fawr). In 1325, after her brother, King Charles IV, had seized Edward's possess-ions in France, she paid a visit to the French court, ostensibly to act as intermediary, but actually to gather an army against her husband. Mortimer and Isabella cut a swathe through southern England (supported by the new Earl of Lancaster, another of Edward's cousins), and contrived to have the king abdicate. When months of ill treatment in miserable confinement failed to finish him off, they arranged his murder. Both Despensers were also treated to humiliating and painful public executions.

Ironically, it was in south Wales that Edward fell into the hands of his enemies. A memorial at Pant-y-brâd, near Llantrisant, purports to mark the exact spot where he was captured on 16 November 1326. The name Pant-y-brâd means 'valley of treachery'. This is the nearest thing we have to evidence that something happened there, and the name implies some loyalty to Edward on the part of his Welsh subjects. The deposed king was taken to Berkeley Castle in Gloucestershire, where he met his horrific death, and he is buried in Gloucester Cathedral.

His own son had, in the meantime, grown into a more promising leader. Edward III was not, however, Prince of Wales; the title was still a novelty, and did not automatically belong to him in his capacity as heir to the throne. Soon after achieving his majority, the young king disposed of Mortimer and Isabella and began ruling independently. Mortimer was ignominiously executed by hanging, and Isabella spent the rest of her life in forcible seclusion. By yet another twist of fate, a descendant and namesake of Mortimer's would be recognized as heir to the throne by the childless Richard II in 1385.

Before long, Edward III had married and was himself a father several times over. It is with *his* eldest son, another Edward (more familiarly known to us as the Black Prince) that many of the traditions relating to the title of Prince of Wales first made their appearance.

The Black Prince with King John of Bohemia, from whom he is thought to have inherited his emblem of three feathers. A fantasy scene from a Victorian print.

Edward of Woodstock and Richard of Bordeaux

No doubt many Welsh people have wondered how the Prince of Wales came to have ostrich feathers as his emblem, since even a well-travelled Welshman of the Middle Ages could have had no expectation of seeing a live ostrich. The emblem, and the motto that go with it, really have nothing to do with Wales, but are a historical accident.

Edward, the eldest son of King Edward III, was born on 15 June 1330, at Woodstock Palace near Oxford, a building that stood on the site now occupied by Blenheim Palace. Edward of Woodstock, or the Black Prince as he is almost always called (though he was not called this during his lifetime), spent virtually no time in Wales, apart from a quick trip to Chester to look for archers for his army; but there is some evidence that he valued his title, if only for the revenues it brought him. After a glorious military career that began when he was a teenager, he spent a large proportion of his mature years in Aquitaine, providing a nominal presence on his father's behalf, to discourage those who might have been considering taking advantage of their over-lord's physical absence. Prince of Aquitaine was one of the Black Prince's titles, and at this time was probably considered more significant than the title of Prince of Wales.

In 1337 the prince was given the Earldom of Chester, one of the titles that had been created by William the Conqueror to encourage his henchmen to help him subdue the Welsh Marches. It had reverted to the Crown a century earlier, in 1237 (its last holder, John de Scotia, having been the husband of Llywelyn the Great's daughter Elen), and had been held by the first three King Edwards. At the same time, Edward of Woodstock obtained the Duchy of Cornwall.

The Prince of Wales was invested with his newest title in 1343, just short of his tenth birthday. Like his predecessor, Edward II, he was invested at a session of Parliament, this time in Westminster Hall. Also like his predecessor, he received an oath of fealty from his subjects throughout the principality. It is known that the prince was presented with a *sertum*, a kind of coronet, as part of his princely regalia; his predecessor may also have had one, but there is no record of this. The Black Prince's 'gold circlet' later passed to his younger brother, who already owned a similar one from his own creation as Duke of Clarence. Precedents for the investiture ceremonies of more recent Princes of Wales were thus already in place.

A council had been appointed to assist Edward of Caernarfon in the government of Wales and his other territories. The new council created for the Black Prince had twelve members, and there are documentary records of its proceedings. Its activities seem to have been more extensive than those of its predecessor body. It acted as the ultimate court of appeal in legal disputes, and proved useful when resources were needed to support the prince's military campaigning.

The charter of 1301 had defined the boundaries of the principality, but this was subject to change depending on the whims of successive monarchs. In 1343, the king sent a commissioner to take possession of the lands in question and 'deliver' them to the prince. This reference is to a kind of census by which the king could assess the current value of the principality and calculate the revenues due to his son in future – a useful opportunity for such an exercise, at which no subject could reasonably take offence. Nevertheless, the commissioners met with token resistance at Builth, and were obliged to take the castle by force and place its occupants in custody until the 'misunderstanding' was sorted out. This was an exception; in general, their mission was accomplished smoothly.

Revenues from Wales came in the form of rents, fines, fees and other dues, but the prince did not receive them automatically along with his title. They belonged to the Crown, and in years to come they would sometimes be seen as a way for rulers to bring errant sons into line. Additional funds might be forthcoming as a good-will gesture. The more wealthy of the Black Prince's new tenants were invited to make a 'gift' to their

overlord in recognition of his new status. Not everyone responded favourably to this suggestion. Welsh tenants knew the true
reason for the request, and were reluctant to make a contribution
towards the cost of the upkeep of the English-built castles.

Throughout Edward of Woodstock's tenure of the title, there
would be occasions when his Welsh tenants disagreed publicly
about the nature and extent of their liabilities towards him. In
1347, for example, the diocese of St David's maintained its
independence of him and took the matter to law, eventually
winning its case ten years later. Welsh landowners might also
come under the authority of the Prince of Wales in respect of
their estates *outside* the principality, and these included the
Welsh bishops. Nevertheless, Edward's income from the principality showed a marked increase over receipts for the preceding
period.

It is to the Black Prince that the Prince of Wales owes his
emblem, the three ostrich feathers, and its accompanying motto,
'Ich dien', meaning 'I serve'. There remains some mystery about
how Edward came by them. He is said to have inherited both
from the blind King John of Bohemia, against whom he fought
at the Battle of Crécy. (The king had to be strapped between two
other knights in order to participate.) It is said by some that
Edward chose the emblem after seeing the king's dead body on
the battlefield, symbolic as it seemed to him of a particular brand
of courage. Other sources suggest that he killed the king himself
and snatched a plume from his helmet. The latter explanation
seems to go against the code of honour prevalent in the Hundred
Years War. A living king would have been good for a large ransom,
whilst the dead body of a blind man would not have been much
of a battle trophy.

However, there was also a history of the use of ostrich feathers
as an emblem within the family of the prince's mother, Philippa
of Hainault. All we can say for certain is that the prince and his
wife, Joan of Kent, both used ostrich feathers on seals and other
items, and that his uncle, Edward of York, is known to have used
the motto, 'Ich dien', which cannot have originated from
Hainault. Whatever the truth, it is more than likely that these
trappings were taken on as a mark of respect for the indomitable
spirit of the late King John, rather than with any thought of
their becoming indissolubly linked with the principality.

The prince's army at Crécy included a contingent of Welsh archers, men whom he had personally recruited on visits to the border country. When they joined the English in battle, they were given a green-and-white uniform to wear. The average English soldier would not have found it easy to distinguish between the Welsh and French languages, and no doubt the short, dark Welshmen *looked* equally foreign.

Not long after his marriage to his cousin, the already twice married Joan of Kent, Edward of Woodstock was dispatched by his father to Aquitaine, the other royal possession of which he was titular prince. Edward III had inherited, or conquered, huge swathes of French territory, claiming the kingdom by right of his mother, Isabella of France, sister of three French kings (all of whom had died without leaving a male heir). The French, not surprisingly, rejected his claim, quoting Salic law, and offered the throne instead to Philippe of Valois. It was therefore incumbent on the English king to maintain a strong presence on French soil.

In Aquitaine, the Black Prince and his princess lived in luxurious style, holding court alternately at Angoulême and at Bordeaux, where their younger son, the future Richard II, was born. Joan was much criticized for her love of splendour, and the prince was no better in that respect, ostentatious generosity being an integral part of the code of chivalry he chose to adopt. Ruling the region on his father's behalf, however, also entailed dealing with unrest, and the prince spent significant periods away from his family, campaigning in difficult and dangerous conditions. This took its toll on his health, and in 1371, after a long and ultimately fruitless campaign in support of the king's ally, Pedro the Cruel of Castile, he made up his mind to return to England, admitting defeat. He declared that he could no longer carry out his duties.

Pedro was father-in-law to two of Edward's sisters, so it was in the family's interests to support him, even though his standards of chivalry were not those of the Prince of Wales. The Black Prince's army had to march through the Pyrenees in the depths of winter to reach their destination. The Battle of Najera in 1367 restored Pedro to the throne of Castile, and once again it was Wales's trusty longbowmen who made all the difference to the result. Then began the disagreements. Pedro was slow to deliver the promised rewards, and the only way to pay off the army was to levy higher taxes back home in Aquitaine. Edward was suffering from dropsy when a French army arrived to take advantage of his weakness. He defeated them too, and the town of Limoges was taken, sacked and the inhabitants put to the sword. As though in judgement on the prince for this savagery, his elder son, named Edward after him, died shortly afterwards. Pedro the Cruel also died, in March 1369, never having repaid his allies for their assistance.

The prince had taken the decision to return to England permanently. He was in no physical condition for further fighting. Despite this, a year later he was preparing to go back to France, the situation having worsened considerably in his absence. Fortunately for his family, rough weather prevented him setting sail, and it was at this point that he made up his mind to give up the principality of Aquitaine once and for all, since he no longer had the strength to hold it for the king. The prince and princess set up home again at Berkhamsted Castle, which they preferred to their grander London residences.

Around the same time, a rival claimant to the title of Prince of Wales was making his presence felt, in Europe if not in England. Owain Lawgoch ('Owain of the Red Hand'), or, as the French called him, Yvain de Galles, was descended from Llywelyn Fawr through Rhodri ap Gruffydd, the younger brother of Llywelyn the Last. This gave Owain Lawgoch a tenuous claim to be the rightful heir of the royal house of Gwynedd, and entitled his supporters to call him 'mab darogan' or 'son of prophecy'. Huge numbers of people can claim descent from Llywelyn Fawr, but mostly in the female line, which in the Middle Ages was ignored by the Welsh, as it was by the French. Owain's abortive attempt at an invasion, in 1372, made little impact. Not long afterwards, he was murdered by his own squire, and that put an end, at least temporarily, to any idea of a rival prince setting himself up against the official claimant. (A society exists to celebrate Owain Lawgoch's memory, and he is included with other Welsh princes in the memorial garden at Pennal, near Machynlleth.) As we shall see, however, he was not the last to use his royal blood in support of his claim on the principality.

When he knew he was dying, the Black Prince must have been just as anxious for his surviving son's welfare and position as he had ever been for his own. He suggested allowing the title of Prince of Wales to pass to Richard, and Edward III, devastated at losing his eldest and most promising son at such an early age, was only too ready to agree to the idea. Once again, this may be seen as a mere gesture to honour the dead, rather than an indication that Wales had any significance in the greater order. Richard of Bordeaux was immediately recognized as heir to the throne. He took his father's title of Prince of Wales in recognition of this and for no other reason.

The Black Prince is buried in Canterbury Cathedral, as opposed to one of the more traditional resting-places of English kings, for reasons going back to a vow he had made to the Pope in return for the dispensation that had allowed him to marry his cousin fifteen years earlier. The prince had fulfilled his promise to build a chapel in the cathedral crypt, and expressed a wish to be buried there, perhaps in a growing awareness that he would never make it to the throne. When the time came, it was decided that this was not a prominent enough position for his tomb, and instead he was placed in the nave of the cathedral, where his effigy can still be seen. The 'black' armour has now turned a shiny bronze as a result of vigorous cleaning. It is the best idea we will ever have of what he really looked like.

Edward's widow, Joan of Kent (herself a descendant of Llywelyn Fawr), got one-third of the principality's revenues, small compensation for the loss of both husband and social status but perhaps generous when one considers that there was no precedent for dealing with the widow of a Prince of Wales. This settlement on her meant that her son, Richard, would, during her lifetime, receive only two-thirds of the Black Prince's lands. St David's, where the clergy had rebelled against the Black Prince's authority, was a notable omission from the lands granted to his son.

Richard spent only a year as Prince of Wales, and had little time to put his stamp on the title. Nevertheless, it is significant that he carried it, becoming only the third prince officially to do so. Edward III was sixty-four when the Black Prince died on 8 June 1376, and himself passed away a year later, leaving the throne to his ten-year-old grandson. Richard proved an un-popular king, and was destined to lose the throne that had been so strengthened by the reign of his distinguished predecessor.

Even after acceding to the throne, the young Richard spent most of his time at Kennington Palace, where he lived with his widowed mother. It was a sheltered existence, allowing the government to be run by experienced adults. A boy king had not been seen in England since the Norman conquest, and it was probably by staying out of the limelight that Richard was able to survive to manhood. In 1381, he was forced to make a rare public appearance by the crisis of the Peasants' Revolt, an incident regarded as something of a watershed in English history. Although the regents (led by Richard's uncle, John of Gaunt) had maintained order in the country, they had not shown much sympathy with the peasants of the southern counties, who hoped to gain something by marching on London, egged on by a renegade priest named John Ball and a demagogue called Wat Tyler.

King Richard II's encounter with the peasants was a major public–relations coup for the young king, but in the end the rebels dispersed in disorder and their leaders were executed. Tyler escaped with a swift beheading. Richard, young as he was, was present in person to watch John Ball being hung, drawn and quartered. It was part of the toughening-up process essential for a successful ruler.

Having shown some diplomatic ability, the next logical step was for Richard to take on the reins of government in earnest. To prove himself further, he needed a queen. The following year he was married, to Anne, daughter of King Charles IV of Bohemia (Charles was the son and heir of blind King John). Aged sixteen, Anne was six months older than Richard himself, and they remained happily married for twelve years, though they had no children. We may speculate on the reasons for the failure to produce an heir, but we can never know for certain. All sources are agreed that the couple were almost blissfully happy, and that Richard was devastated by Anne's death, from plague, in 1394.

Richard was not as successful a king as he seems to have been a husband. The nobles' discontent grew, fired by two aspects of his conduct: his reliance on a few favourites, and his policy of peace, which had led to the loss of military superiority over the French. The 'Lords Appellant', led by another of Richard's uncles, Thomas of Woodstock, and including his cousin, Henry Bolingbroke, wanted their say in government, and were prepared to go to arms against the king. It was only through the intervention of the popular John of Gaunt that Richard II was able to retain power.

Richard's relationship with Wales was a strong one. Both he and his father had been Princes of Wales and had recruited Welshmen into their armies. As king, Richard actually spent some time in the principality, venturing across the border from Chester in 1387 in search of good men to add to his personal retinue. In 1397, he raised the status of the city of Chester, giving it control of the neighbouring Welsh region we now know as Flintshire. He passed through Wales, both north and south, on his way to and from Ireland, and it was in north Wales that he was finally captured by his enemies. This close contact with its nominal prince is one of the historical reasons for the Welsh support of the Yorkist cause during the Wars of the Roses. It was not until Pembroke-born Henry Tudor became the Lancastrian heir seventy years later that the Welsh wholeheartedly switched their allegiance.

In order to understand the momentous events of the coming year, 1400, it is necessary to examine the latter years of Richard's reign. His heirless state was never a satisfactory situation for a reigning king; but Richard was still in his prime. Anne of Bohemia's replacement as queen, Isabelle of Valois, was younger still and looked likely to deliver what the nation expected of her, if only her husband could maintain his hold on the throne for long enough.

Richard, despite his success in quelling the Peasants' Revolt of 1481, lacked the common touch. He dabbled in politics without retaining control of government. Bolingbroke, the son of the supportive uncle John of Gaunt, was only one of many who undermined the king's authority. Richard exiled Bolingbroke, and confiscated his lands, but did not take out his anger on his cousin's family; Bolingbroke's son, the future Henry V, would later show signs of admiration for Richard (who was the boy's godfather). Meanwhile, in an attempt to secure the succession, he named the Marcher lord, Roger Mortimer (a descendant of the man who had been responsible for the death of Edward II), as heir presumptive. If Richard died childless, Mortimer would take the throne. When Roger Mortimer was killed at the Battle of Kells in 1398, his young son, Edmund, replaced him as nominal heir.

Richard of Bordeaux, Prince of Wales after his father's death and later King Richard II. From a Victorian print.

The following year, Richard was in Wales, having landed in Haverfordwest on his way back from Ireland and travelled north as far as Conwy, when he encountered the emissaries of the man who planned to usurp his crown. Bolingbroke had arrived back in the country, with an army, while Richard was absent. Both Richard and his rival had support within Wales. Richard had been Prince of Wales, albeit briefly, as had his father before him, and in his entourage were members of the Tudor family. Although Henry could claim no such distinction, he was one of Wales's most powerful landowners. The lordship of Brecon brought him extensive estates within the principality. His first wife, Mary de Bohun, was the daughter of Humphrey de Bohun, Earl of Hereford. This evened up the odds. Richard and Henry met face to face at Flint. Richard was taken into custody and was deemed to have abdicated. The promises made to obtain his surrender – that he would be treated with dignity – were broken. He was removed from the sympathetic environment of north Wales and taken to Pontefract Castle in Yorkshire, where he is reputed to have been starved to death.

Henry IV took the throne on 30 September 1399, beginning the Lancastrian dynasty, so named after his father, John of Gaunt, who had been Duke of Lancaster. Henry's eldest son, Henry of Monmouth, was invested as Prince of Wales a month later, re-inforcing his father's kingship. This heightens the significance of the actions of Owain Glyndŵr, less than a year later, in proclaiming himself the rightful Prince of Wales.

Henry of Monmouth

One of the most dashing Princes of Wales was also one of the most famous English kings. Bolingbroke's son, also named Henry, had been born in Wales, late in the summer of 1387, at Monmouth, a castle in the possession of his mother's family, the Bohuns. Mary de Bohun died when her son was only six, but she left behind her the legacy of Norman-Welsh relations, the Normans of south Wales having been among the most quickly integrated in the whole country.

Despite the early upset of losing his mother, Henry grew into a fine soldier, unlike his often-ailing father. The relationship between the two was fraught with difficulty, a pattern that is common between fathers and sons worldwide and which would repeat itself over and over through the history of the title of Prince of Wales (some would say right up to the present day). Henry Bolingbroke usurped the throne from his cousin Richard in 1399. Two days after his coronation, his twelve-year-old son was invested as Prince of Wales with the approval of Parliament. By the time he was sixteen, he was a seasoned soldier.

The king's hold on the throne was largely based on his son's military brilliance, as a reward for which the younger Henry was made President of the Council at the age of twenty one. Nevertheless, Shakespeare does not stretch the truth too far when, in *Henry IV Part II*, he has the dying king say to his son: 'Thy life did manifest thou lovedst me not, And thou wilt have me die assured of it.' In 1411, the king, temporarily in good spirits, dispersed the 'Prince's friends', an oligarchy that had dominated the government for the past year, and took away his son's position as a privy councillor.

Henry of Monmouth, later King Henry V.
From a Victorian print.

Yet Henry, even in his youth, can hardly have been the jack-the-lad that Shakespeare made him out to be. A soldier of his ability could not have been created without some understanding of discipline. There was plenty of opportunity for Henry to 'try his spurs' just as his great-great-uncle, the Black Prince, had done. England was at war again – this time with Wales. The rebel leader, Owain Glyndŵr, had no difficulty in persuading the French to back his claim to the title of Prince of Wales. Glyndŵr even held parliaments, and set up court at Harlech, one of Edward I's well-designed stone castles, perched high on a rock above Cardigan Bay. It had never been intended for occupation by a Welsh garrison. It was fitting that Glyndŵr's downfall should partly have been engineered by his rival, a prince whose qualities made him equally worthy of the title.

At the Battle of Shrewsbury in 1403 (the battle in which Harry Hotspur met his end), the teenager was severely wounded by an arrow that entered his cheek. The royal surgeon, John Bradmore, was obliged to invent a special device to enable him to remove the head of the arrow without doing further damage, and succeeded miraculously. Henry was undoubtedly left with a scar on his face, which may explain why the best-known portrait of him is in profile. He certainly looked nothing like Laurence Olivier or Kenneth Branagh, nor would he have dreamed of appearing bareheaded in battle as is sometimes required for dramatic purposes.

Most of the legends about the youth of Henry V are bogus. It is true that he was often in financial difficulties, but much of this was due to the need to pay off his army. It is also true that he could hardly wait to attain the throne. On his accession, he began to behave in a manner he is said to have learned from his ill-fated uncle, Richard II (whose body he arranged to have brought back to London for burial in Westminster Abbey). Richard had kept his godson in gentle custody during Bolingbroke's exile, and had even taken him on his military campaign to Ireland. When he came to the throne, Henry stopped all carousing and womanizing (if indeed he had ever indulged in these habits), had his hair cut in a monkish style, devoted himself to kingly pursuits, and adopted an orthodox religious fervour. Moreover, he appeared to take his claim to the throne of France very seriously indeed.

Perhaps it was because of his success in subduing Wales and bringing it back under Plantagenet rule that Henry V began to look abroad for his next challenge. Having come to the throne, he offered a pardon to Owain Glyndŵr, who had now gone to ground; by this action he neutralized any remaining opposition from that quarter. The French, on the other hand, had supported Glyndŵr when the latter had sought to take away the prince's title to Wales, and this was a good enough reason for Henry to strike back and snatch at a kingdom that was, technically, his. His claim centred on his descent from Isabella, the estranged wife of Edward II, through Henry's great-grandfather, Edward III. Since the magnificent campaigns of Edward and his son, the Black Prince, however, much of France had been lost to the enemy. Aquitaine, proudly held by the Black Prince as a principality, had reverted to a mere dukedom.

Not everyone wanted the war, and not everyone loved Henry. As described so dramatically in the early scenes of Shakespeare's play, a conspiracy to assassinate the king was discovered just as the fighting force was preparing to leave from Southampton. Its leaders included Lord Scrope (a man Henry had counted among his closest friends) and Richard, Earl of Cambridge, another descendant of Edward III. Both were executed on 5 August 1415, before the army set sail.

The decision to try and invade France might seem to have been unwise, but that was not exactly what Henry intended when he attacked Harfleur in September 1415. He might have consolidated his small gains and retreated to England in good order, had it not been for the series of misfortunes that resulted in the loss of the better part of his army. Depleted and disillusioned, the soldiers marched unwillingly north in an attempt to draw the French away from Harfleur. Their progress was too slow, and they found themselves obliged to face the enemy at the little village of Azincourt in the Pas de Calais – following Henry's unsuccessful attempt to bargain for his life with King Charles VI of France.

It is now well known that the victory of 'Agincourt' (as the English chose to spell it) was no more than a fluke. The role of the longbowmen, however, was as vital as history describes it. The longbow tradition in Wales was firmly founded. It was their flurry of arrows that delayed the charging French knights long enough for them to flounder and suffocate in the mud. That a good proportion of the fighting force was Welsh is reflected in Shakespeare's decision to include 'Fluellen' (clearly based on a mispronunciation of 'Llywelyn') as a cast member, and he has Henry V himself say, in response to a query from Ancient Pistol: 'No, I am a Welshman.' It is worth pausing to note that Henry's birthplace and its location were evidently known to the playwright. Despite Henry's defeat of Glyndŵr, he was never ashamed of his own Welsh blood and birth. Welshmen fought for him at Azincourt, including 'Davy Gam', who had been a sworn enemy of Owain Glyndŵr and was for some years imprisoned by the latter. Gam was one of relatively few notable men who lost their lives in the battle.

The fact is, though, that Wales was no longer regarded as a separate country. Henry of Monmouth could well have said 'I am a Welshman' in real life, but it would have meant no more than it would if the present Prince of Wales were to say, 'I am a Londoner.' Having a strong hold on England and Wales, and having relinquished the title of Prince of Wales (which now lay dormant, Henry being as yet unmarried), he had turned his attention outward, to France, and the victory at Azincourt gained him some unlooked-for privileges. Charles VI, having lost the flower of his army, including a huge proportion of the French nobility, sued for a temporary peace.

This was not the end of the war with France. Henry spent some of the intervening period strengthening the nation's sea power, driving out the Genoese, France's allies, who had been threatening the waters of the English Channel. Luckily for him, France had internal problems, with John 'the Fearless', Duke of Burgundy, seizing Paris, and Bernard VII, Count of Armagnac, busy promoting the interests of his own little empire. Rouen fell to Henry almost without a struggle. While all this was going on, Henry joined other European leaders in supporting the election of Pope Martin V, which ended the 'great schism' within the Roman Catholic Church. In 1419, John the Fearless was assassinated by accomplices of the dauphin, causing his heir, Philip 'the Good' of Burgundy, to form an alliance with Henry. In the following year, 'mad' King Charles VI acknowledged Henry as his heir and offered him his young daughter, Katherine of Valois, as his bride.

Charles's eldest daughter, Isabelle (the widow of King Richard II), had already turned down the chance to marry the English king, who was the same age as herself. Even by 1420, Isabelle's little sister Katherine was hardly a worthy consort, being only eighteen to Henry's thirty-two years, but by the end of 1421 she had given birth to a son and heir. The dauphin, however, refused to give up his claim to the French throne without a fight. Henry V, in the course of another military campaign, sickened and died of dysentery or marsh fever, an ignominious end for such a great military leader. Katherine lost her husband, her position as consort, and the care of her baby son, who became King Henry VI at less than one year of age.

Owain Glyndŵr

Although the title which forms the theme for this book came into existence only at the moment Wales was losing its independence, it would be unreasonable to deny Owain Glyndŵr as much space as any of its post-Conquest holders. Not only is he regarded by many as the last 'true' Prince of Wales, but he was recognized as such, in his own lifetime, by the King of France among others. The fact that he lived contemporaneously with an 'official' Prince of Wales does not lessen the strength of his claim, even if he is not listed by Buckingham Palace among past holders of the title.

In the opening chapters of his book, *The Revolt of Owain Glyn Dŵr*, R. R. Davies gives a detailed pen-picture of what life in Wales may have been like in the years leading up to 1400. Although north Wales had been under English rule for over a hundred years (and parts of south Wales for more than twice as long), there was not exactly an atmosphere of oppression. Norman overlords had intermarried with the Welsh aristocracy. The Welsh language was still being spoken in Herefordshire, Shropshire and other border areas. Rebellion was the last thing on the mind of the average peasant, who was too busy scraping a living to care much whether the lord of the manor was English or Welsh. The group who banded together behind Glyndŵr represented a small, loyal following, and those who followed them into battle were their employees or tenants and had little choice in the matter.

This does not mean that Glyndŵr lacked popular support, only that it needed to be mustered. There was no popular movement to overthrow the Anglo-Norman landlords until the specific incident that rankled enough with Owain to cause him

*Bronze of Owain Glyndŵr by Dave Haynes in the memorial garden
at Pennal. Photo © Deborah Fisher.*

to put himself forward as an alternative leader. There was, however, a group of disgruntled Welsh landowners or 'uchelwyr' who had accumulated enough grounds for resentment to push them over the edge.

Whilst we know the exact dates of birth and death of almost all those Princes of Wales who were heirs to the throne, we can only make a rough guess at those of Owain Glyndŵr. He is thought to have been born around 1354, and the date of his death is even more of a mystery. He may well have lived into his seventies.

Owain's life, and his death (if and when it occurred), are spectacularly worthy of a Prince of Wales. He was born at Glyndyfrdwy in north Wales (from which he took his last name), but one of the earliest official records of his existence is in 1386, when he is listed as a witness in a lawsuit. All the indications are that Owain studied law in his youth, probably at the Inns of Court in London, making him a natural candidate to introduce ideas of freedom, democracy and self-government to his fellow countrymen. It equipped him better for the business of ruling than his predecessors, particularly Llywelyn the Last who had plenty of courage but was not over-burdened with administrative ability. Owain was not, however, descended from Llywelyn the Last (who had no surviving descendants) nor even from Llywelyn Fawr (who had many, one of whom would become Owain's son-in-law). His only link with the royal family of Gwynedd was his claim to be descended from Gruffydd ap Cynan (father of the twelfth-century political and military genius, Owain Gwynedd, and an ancestor of both Llywelyns).

Twenty-five years before Owain Glyndŵr's revolt, another namesake, Owain Lawgoch, had claimed the title of Prince of Wales on the strength of his direct descent from Llywelyn Fawr. Owain Lawgoch had been recognized by the French, but had limited support within Wales, and had been murdered before he could become a real threat to the English king. The political climate had changed in the intervening years, but Owain Lawgoch's minor successes were not forgotten.

The English Princes of Wales have never attempted to rule the country in any true sense; at most, they have attempted a symbiotic relationship with their principality. For Owain Glyndŵr, the titles 'prince' and 'king' were synonymous, and he underlined this by calling his own parliaments at Machynlleth and Harlech. No comparable assembly had been called in Wales since the reign of Hywel Dda in the ninth century – and Owain's parliaments were the last until the National Assembly was created in 1999.

In Owain's tenure, the title of Prince of Wales had a completely different meaning from the one it had when held by princes who were heirs to the English throne. Owain Glyndŵr was a mature man, not a fledgeling prince, and his plan was to rule Wales, not simply to take its revenues and act as a figurehead. Whether he would have been a good or effective ruler is hard to say. He did not actually administer the country, even at the height of his success; there was still an Anglo-Norman administration alongside his 'government', acting almost as a failsafe. When Owain's grip slackened, there were plenty of people standing by to take over again.

Owain Glyndŵr's rebellion began, nominally, as the result of a dispute between himself and Reginald Grey of Ruthin, whom later generations have chosen to depict as the archetype of the arrogant Norman overlord. The causes of the dispute are vague, and it seems out of all proportion that the Welsh should choose this particular controversy as the cue for an attempt to overthrow English rule. In fact, as we have seen, the outbreak of violence had much to do with the prevailing political climate. The displacement of Richard II as king was the real catalyst. It is not hard to believe that Owain Glyndŵr had always had an ambition to take over where his forefathers left off, and had merely been waiting for a suitable opportunity.

At first, it looked unlikely he would get far. After a year, the revolt's momentum appeared to be exhausted, and the English confidently withdrew some of the extra forces they had put in place to counter the rebellion. Henry IV may have been a clever man, but he was no diplomat. His biggest political mistake of 1402 was his failure to ransom young Edmund Mortimer, previously his loyal servant. Owain Glyndŵr's men had captured Mortimer at the Battle of Bryn Glas, thinking him a valuable hostage. The king, however, noted that Mortimer, having the blood of both the Welsh and English royal families in his veins, was a potential trouble-maker and decided he was best left where he was.

Mortimer did not waste much time in taking his revenge. He, too, saw the possibilities of the situation, and allowed himself to be turned, marrying Owain's daughter, Catrin, and joining the revolt. By the end of the year, his uncle, Sir Edmund Mortimer, was writing to his associates with the news that:

> Oweyn Glyndwr has raised a quarrel of which the object is, if King Richard be alive, to restore him to his crown; and if not that, my honoured nephew, who is the right heir to the said crown, shall be King of England, and that the said Oweyn will assert his right in Wales.

No doubt Owain knew full well that Richard II was already dead, but his stated purpose added an air of respectability to his case.

This in itself would have been a serious enough reverse for Henry IV, but he surely could not have foreseen the knock-on effect. Another of his loyal henchmen, Henry Percy the younger, or 'Harry Hotspur' as he is better remembered, was getting rather tired of his king's failure to recognize his own contribution to the war effort. Percy and his father had done useful service as royal lieutenants in Wales, but their efforts to make peace with the rebels did not win them any approval. Hotspur's motives are not clear-cut. The brother-in-law of Edmund Mortimer, he was in collusion with Owain Glyndŵr even before he officially turned traitor in 1403. Together with Glyndŵr and Mortimer, he entered into an agreement to share the country three ways after the anticipated defeat and deposition of Henry IV.

Things could so easily have gone the other way, and we can only speculate on whether Hotspur would have turned against the Welsh prince in time, just as he had turned against the English king. His hour never came; he died at Shrewsbury within a short time of entering into the three-way agreement (the 'Tripartite Indenture'), leaving Glyndŵr once again without outside assistance. This did not end the rebellion, though. In 1404, Glyndŵr went through a form of coronation, in front of representatives sent by the Scottish, French and Castilian governments.

Glyndŵr sometimes referred to himself as 'mab darogan' or 'son of prophecy', and it is worth going into more detail on this concept. The expression seems to hark back to the misty days of Myrddin or Merlin, the legendary figure we nowadays associate with King Arthur. The real Myrddin was probably a contemporary of Gwrtheyrn or Vortigern, the fifth–century British chieftain. Perhaps it was he who originated 'canu brud' ('prophetic singing'), a whole literary genre. Several medieval writers refer back to Myrddin's prophecies, but the first specific reference to 'mab darogan' is in a poem addressed to Llywelyn Fawr by one of his bards, Prydydd y Moch, in the early thirteenth century. This type of Messianic prophecy is common to many cultures over many centuries, and it is impossible to tell whether the Welsh merely borrowed the idea from elsewhere.

In his poem, Prydydd y Moch says that a king will come to throw off the Saxon yoke from Wales, and that he will be 'o hil eryron o Eryri', a descendant of the eagles of Snowdonia. Thus, Glyndŵr's descent from the princes of Gwynedd gave him the right to consider himself a claimant to the role. It was even rumoured that he ate of the eagle's flesh in order to consolidate his claim. A shooting star seen in 1402 gave him additional credibility.

The year 1406 finds Owain Glyndŵr corresponding with King Charles VI of France (this of course was nearly ten years before the mad monarch's ambitions were dashed at Agincourt). In a house called Cefn Caer (because of its position on the former site of a Roman camp), Owain wrote the famous document whose return to Wales has been the subject of a long-running campaign. 'May the son of the glorious virgin long preserve your majesty,' he tells King Charles, laying out his plans for his country's future, which include a renewed loyalty to the Pope, the provision of Welsh-speaking clergy, and the founding of two universities, one in north and one in south Wales. In addition, he asks Charles to ensure that Henry of Lancaster and his followers (Owain is thought to have been one during the 1390s) are branded heretics and appropriately punished. The Pennal letter, as it is called, languished for centuries in the Bibliothèque Nationale, Paris, almost as though waiting to rise again from the ashes when Wales was ready to receive it.

This 'Pennal policy' as it is sometimes known, is generally seen as the formulation of Owain's grand plan for Wales. In reality, however, by the time it was written in 1406, Owain's power was already on the wane. The public statement of his intentions was an act of desperation. The French had given as

*Cefn Caer, the house where Owain Glyndŵr wrote the Pennal letter.
Photo © Deborah Fisher.*

much practical assistance as they would ever do. By declaring his allegiance to Avignon's renegade Pope, Owain hoped to remain in their good books and to obtain further military aid. King Charles was losing interest. He had hoped that Owain's rebellion would permanently undermine the English government, whilst presenting no threat to France. With Owain in control of much of Wales and keeping the English army occupied, there was little to be gained in spending any more money on him. Charles VI had other fish to fry.

What the Pennal letter does prove is that Owain had thought about the future. Not only did he have the literacy and the legal training to set down his ideas on paper (and with his senate around him, including English- and French-speaking diplomats like Gruffydd Yonge, he had plenty of administrative support), but he recognized that it was not enough to win

Wales from the English by military means. He would have to be its ruler in every respect, and he was astute enough to foresee that this might mean unpopularity at times; hence the need for powerful allies when the tide turned. Perhaps, indeed, he had already learned the lesson from what was going on around him.

The medieval church of St Peter ad Vincula stands on the very spot in Pennal where Owain held his last known senate meeting. The only church of its name in Wales, it may have been so designated in competition with Henry IV's royal chapel in the Tower of London. Visitors to Pennal can now pay their respects to the Welsh princes in a special memorial garden, where a bronze statue of Owain holds pride of place on its pedestal.

That the career of one Prince of Wales should have been cut short by the military prowess of another, junior, holder of the title is ironic. It was probably plague that struck down Edmund Mortimer in about 1409; but it was Henry of Monmouth, long before the days of Agincourt, who harried Glyndŵr's army, laid siege to his strongholds, and captured his wife and children. Their fate is not definitely known, though there are records of the funerals of Catrin and several of her children. As for Glyndŵr himself, his final days are shrouded in even greater mystery.

By 1413, Owain's utopian rule was over, and the man himself had disappeared. It is now generally accepted that he retreated to a manor in Herefordshire, owned by his son-in-law and loyal supporter, Sir John Scudamore, and that the king, for whatever reason, elected not to pursue him there. Thousands of people had lost their lives as a result of Glyndŵr's rebellion; but in the end, he did not die violently. Naturally, some say the son of prophecy never died at all, but is still waiting, like King Arthur, to come to the rescue of his nation when the time calls for it. He might be along any day now.

A Tragic Youth

Edward of Westminster's life was a short one, but he does have one distinction, unlikely ever to be equalled. He was the only Prince of Wales to die in battle, an amazing statistic given the habits of kings' sons during the Middle Ages. We have come fifty years on from the investiture of Henry of Monmouth. King Henry V's son, yet another Henry, was a baby when his father died of fever while campaigning in France. The child's mother, Katherine of Valois, was the daughter of the French king, Charles VI, and was only twenty at the time she gave birth. A few months later, her husband, Henry V, was dead and she became an outcast from the court. Because of her French blood, she was considered an unsuitable person to bring up the King of England, infant though he was, and she was completely deprived of the opportunity to care for her own child. As for her son, though designated Duke of Cornwall at birth, as is normal with that title, the period in which he was heir to the throne was so brief (he became king at the age of nine months) that he was never styled Prince of Wales.

When, in later years, Henry VI bestowed earldoms on Katherine's other children, his half-brothers, it appears he was attempting to make amends. It was too late for his mother, who had died at the age of thirty-seven without ever fully enjoying a maternal relationship with her eldest son. Whether the forcible separation and lack of maternal bonding affected Henry's mental health is hard to judge, but he grew into a pious, peace-loving man quite unsuited to be king, and not well suited for marriage either. The bride selected for him was Margaret of Anjou, later to be known as the 'Tigress of France' because of her determination not to allow her husband to give away his son's inheritance. Quite different from her predecessor, Edward II's Queen Isabella, Margaret is nevertheless often confused with her.

In the struggle between England and France, the French were getting the upper hand again, and most of the possessions that Henry V had struggled to retain were lost during the early years of his son's reign. Nor did Henry VI have a firm grasp on his own kingdom. It took eight years of marriage for Margaret to produce the couple's only child, a son. Edward was born at Westminster in October 1453, and rumours soon spread that the king was not his father. These rumours, if not the invention of the growing Yorkist movement, certainly worked in the Yorkists' favour.

Richard, Duke of York, who had rather a good claim on the throne (his father having been that same Richard, Earl of Cambridge, who had been executed for treason by Henry V) was a better leader and a more determined man than King Henry VI. He drew much of his support from Wales. York was made protector of the kingdom while Henry was incapacitated by a period of mental illness (it was thought that he might have inherited this tendency from his mother's father, King Charles VI of France). On the king's recovery, the young Prince Edward, who had been formally created Prince of Wales almost as soon as he was born, was invested as such during a session of Parliament. Though not yet two years old, he wore a circlet and a gold ring during the ceremony, and carried a golden rod.

In spite of this gesture of recognition, Henry VI was soon persuaded to recognize the Duke of York's rights as heir in place of the Prince of Wales. In 1460, the principality and all other estates associated with the heir of the throne were given up to the duke, and only the title of Prince of Wales remained with young Edward. Queen Margaret's response was to fight back, and the result was the Wars of the Roses. At the Battle of Wakefield, Margaret defeated the Duke of York and had him executed, along with his seventeen-year-old son, Edmund. The remaining sons fought on, and the result was that Henry lost his throne to Edward, Earl of March, who became King Edward IV at the age of nineteen.

Margaret and the young Edward of Westminster spent literally years on the road. After the Battle of Northampton, which they lost, they journeyed as far west as they could, eventually arriving at the Lancastrian stronghold of Harlech Castle (which only fifty years before had been wrested from Owain Glyndŵr and his Yorkist allies). The queen and her son were forced to flee to France, to the court of her father, René of Anjou. In the course of their travels, they had managed to visit both Wales and Scotland, making Edward of Westminster one of relatively few medieval Princes of Wales to have set foot in his principality.

What was he like, this young man on whom the Lancastrians were now obliged to pin all their hopes? Dulcie M. Ashdown, in her 1979 work, *Princess of Wales*, refers to him as 'a freak', on account of the alleged love of bloodshed instilled in him by his mother. Shakespeare, as one might expect, paints a picture of a saintly youth. The truth is almost certainly somewhere in between. The boy's childhood was worse than unsettled, it was positively nomadic. Prince Edward had been driven out of England (and subsequently out of Wales and Scotland) when Edward IV became king in 1461, after the disastrous Battle of Towton, one of the bloodiest in British history. He had doubtless come to see his mother's homeland, France, as his own, having lived there from the age of ten.

In France, Margaret and Edward finally knew a peaceful existence, without the constant fear of capture. Edward was given a tutor. This teacher, Sir John Fortescue, was at pains to instruct him in the art of kingship, as Fortescue's extant writings show. No doubt Margaret wanted to ensure that her son did not become so settled in France as to forget his destiny. She was determined he should win back his father's crown one day.

Margaret's most valuable ally was one of her husband's half-brothers, Jasper Tudor. Jasper was the second son of Katherine of Valois by her probable secret marriage (she was not allowed by the regents to remarry officially) to a minor Welsh gentle man, Owen Tudor. With Jasper on her side, Margaret hoped to accomplish much, but she was in a stronger position after she received an unexpected approach from Richard Neville, Earl of Warwick, the man we remember as 'Warwick the Kingmaker'. Ten years after his success in grooming Edward IV for the throne, Warwick was out of favour at the English court as a result of the king's ill-considered marriage to the widely detested Elizabeth Woodville.

Warwick arrived in France with an offer for Margaret. If she allowed her son, Prince Edward, to marry his daughter, Anne Neville, he would turn the tables on the wayward king and win back the throne for Henry VI (who was imprisoned in the Tower of London). One way or another, Warwick was determined to have a king for his son-in-law; he had already married off his older daughter, Isabel, to Edward IV's brother, the Duke of Clarence. Margaret was reluctant to trust a man who had been one of the prime movers in stealing her husband's throne in the first place. She recognized, however, that Warwick's military ability was considerable and that she needed him if she was to defeat Edward IV, so she agreed to the deal. Her trust in Warwick was not misplaced; he succeeded in driving Edward IV out of the country, rescued Henry VI from prison and put him back in his rightful place. The time seemed to be ripe for Margaret and her son to return to England so that Edward of Westminster could begin training in earnest to take over his father's shaky throne.

Warwick, military mastermind as he was, lacked political acumen. In the few short months between his victory over Edward IV and the return of the Lancastrian royal family to England, he managed to start a war with Burgundy. The result was that the Burgundians (whose dowager duchess happened to be Edward IV's sister Margaret) lent their support to the Yorkists. In the ensuing Battle of Barnet, Warwick was defeated and killed. Henry VI went straight back to the Tower, where he was promptly murdered, and Margaret arrived in Weymouth with little prospect of regaining her position. Her only hope was to meet up with Jasper Tudor, who was approaching from the Welsh side of the Severn.

The Yorkist and Lancastrian armies met at Tewkesbury. Unable to avail themselves of the promised Tudor support in time, the Lancastrians had no choice but to fight, yet without any real chance of success. Edward of Westminster, Prince of Wales, aged seventeen, had no experience as a military leader, and had to rely on his generals, chief among whom was Edward Beaufort, Duke of Somerset (one of Edward III's descendants on the wrong side of the blanket). They were no match for the Yorkist army, and the battle did not go their way. What happened to the prince is unclear. Some versions of history say he died during the battle, others that he was killed after the event, along with other prisoners. It is well attested that those members of the losing army who sought sanctuary in Tewkesbury Abbey were ruthlessly rooted out by the victors, and most of these lost their lives. Whether Edward, Prince of Wales, was one of them, we cannot be sure. The story that he was murdered by the future Richard III is undoubtedly false, and the tale that he was seen on the battlefield crying out for the Duke of Clarence to come to his aid, though possible, tells us nothing about the manner of his death.

A memorial to Edward may be seen in Tewkesbury Abbey, alongside the tomb of his sister-in-law, Isabel Neville, and her husband, George, Duke of Clarence, best remembered for the legendary manner of his death. Whether Clarence was deliberately drowned in a butt of Malmsey we cannot be sure; what we do know is that such a large container produces fumes that would be enough to render a man unconscious. Clarence had realized his error in going along with Warwick's treason and had been forgiven by his brother, Edward IV; he met his end as punishment for betraying Edward a second time.

The death of Edward of Westminster did not mean even a temporary end to the title, 'Prince of Wales'. For the past few months (for the second time in history), there had been two Princes of Wales at the same time. In fact, there had been two Edwards, each the eldest son of a King of England, and each with the right to call himself by the title. The Edward who continued to hold the title after the Battle of Tewkesbury was no more than a baby. On 2 November 1470, while his father was temporarily off the throne and his mother, Elizabeth Woodville, was left to fend for herself, she had given birth to him in the sanctuary of Westminster Abbey. Because of the proliferation of Edwards, he earned the soubriquet 'Edward of the Sanctuary', in recognition of the circumstances of his birth.

The Curse of the Plantagenets

To give due credit to the usurper Edward IV, he took an active interest in Wales. Despite the activities of the Tudor family in the Wars of the Roses, the bulk of the Welsh had been Yorkist sympathizers, a tendency whose origins could be traced back to Richard II and his father, the Black Prince. Edward 'of the Sanctuary', that treasured son born during the short period of Lancastrian domination in the winter of 1470–1, was invested as Prince of Wales and Earl of Chester at the age of seven months, his father having regained the throne after a brief exile. Edward IV decided that his son, being Prince of Wales, should not merely accept the revenues of the principality, but should actively rule it, in preparation for becoming King of England in due course. In charge of preparing him was the king's brother-in-law, Anthony, Earl Rivers, the brother of Elizabeth Woodville.

There were three first cousins named Edward in this family, so it was a bit crowded. Edward of the Sanctuary, born in 1470, was the eldest. About three years later, his aunt by marriage, Anne Neville, gave birth to a son at Middleham Castle in North Yorkshire. That child's father was Richard, Duke of Gloucester, Edward IV's youngest brother. Then, in 1475, the third surviving Plantagenet brother, George, Duke of Clarence, finally produced a male heir, whom he also named Edward in honour of the king. This boy's mother was none other than Isabel Neville, Anne's sister. Born in Warwick Castle, he became Earl of Warwick on the death of his father in 1478.

Although born into the same family, these three boys were brought up in very different circumstances, in different parts of the country. Edward, Earl of Warwick, was orphaned at the age of three. He was said by some to be simple-minded. His

*Three Plantagenet kings. Edward V, flanked by his father Edward IV
and his uncle Richard III, was the only one to be Prince of Wales.
From a Victorian print.*

father being attainted, he became an earl on the strength of his mother's ancestry. By the time he was ten, he would be a prisoner in the Tower of London, where he remained for the rest of his life. Edward of Middleham, on the other hand, lived a carefree life in his northern home, doted on by both parents and kept away from the bustle of the court and the hassle of politics. No illustrious future was foreseen for either of these double-cousins, closely related through both their mothers and their fathers. In addition, both seemed to have inherited poor health from their Neville mothers, or perhaps from all the inbreeding.

Edward of the Sanctuary, Prince of Wales and heir to the throne of England, was another matter. At the age of three, he was dispatched to Ludlow Castle in the company of his mother and her brother. Earl Rivers appeared a good choice as the child's guardian, a man of education who had been instrumental in the introduction of the printing press to England. His role was to ensure that young Edward received the necessary guidance to make him as good a king as his father. In Ludlow, the prince was eventually to chair the Council of Wales and the Marches. He had been sent, as the eighteenth-century historian David Hume put it, 'that the influence of his presence might overawe the Welsh, and restore the tranquillity of that country'. There were plenty of Welshmen still living who remembered the golden days of Owain Glyndŵr.

In recognition of the prince's arrival, two Welsh counties voted to pay him a special 'tollage'. Edward being a mere toddler, they took this step presumably to curry favour with his father, the king. For the time being, the Council of Wales was in the charge of the royal tutor, the bishop of Worcester, and the prince's great seal was seldom used, except by others on his behalf. His powers and possessions were frequently extended during his time at Ludlow, however, and in 1479 he was given his father's Earldom of March, together with the former Mortimer lands it entailed.

There are records of the regime under which the prince passed his days at Ludlow. Naturally, he did not spend all his time there; in addition to the castle, he was given a country residence, the 'palace' of Tickenhill in the idyllic Worcestershire village of Bewdley (where another Prince of Wales, Arthur Tudor, would later go through a proxy marriage). He is known to have journeyed further west, visiting Wigmore Abbey in Herefordshire, almost on the present-day border. His father, the king, would occasionally call at Ludlow, as he is known to have done in the summer of 1473. Earl Rivers certainly went into Wales on numerous occasions, to administer justice in person at such far-flung places as Pembroke.

By the time the Prince of Wales was five, a bride was being actively sought for him. The first choice was the Infanta Isabella, eldest daughter of the Spanish joint monarchs, Ferdinand and Isabella. Later she was rejected in favour of Anne of Brittany, whose father, Duke Francis II, had no male heir. A provisional date of 1489 was set for the wedding. (When Edward failed to turn up, Anne became the wife of two successive French kings instead.)

It was at Ludlow that Prince Edward was lodged when word reached him of his father's sudden death. Edward IV was only forty years old, but he had lived a life involving not only physical hardship, but also physical excess. Since establishing himself firmly on the throne, Edward had felt no obligation to remain in good physical shape, and had rejected the possibility of giving up his addiction to food, drink and women.

Notwithstanding his stay at Ludlow, it must have been a terrible shock for the king's young son and namesake to hear that his father was dead and the throne was now his. The Prince of Wales was still only twelve, and everyone had thought he would have at least another ten years to prepare for his accession. Personal grief would have been mingled with apprehension about his new role, as well as some excitement at the thought of proceeding to London for his coronation. He was probably too young to anticipate fully the trials that might await him as king.

He returned from Ludlow with a retinue of Welsh followers. Earl Rivers left the party and never saw his nephew again. The prince and his followers were intercepted at Stony Stratford by another of his uncles, Richard, Duke of Gloucester, who had been appointed his 'protector'. Some protector Richard turned out to be. Having disposed of Edward's guard and replaced them with his own men, he set about removing all opposition to his rule. An Italian intelligence agent, Dominic Mancini, who may have met Edward V in person, describes him as an intelligent boy, able to 'discourse elegantly, understand fully, and declaim most excellently'. Mancini writes that 'the Welsh could not bear to think that, owing to their stupidity, their prince had been carried off'. Although his account is mere hearsay, it implies that the title of Prince of Wales was a symbol in which the Welsh had begun to have some confidence.

On the other hand, the Croyland chronicler informs us that:

> armed men in frightening and unheard of numbers were called from the North, from Wales, and from whatever other districts lay within their command and power, and on the 26th day of the same month of June, Richard the Protector claimed for himself the government of the kingdom with the name and title of king.

Evidently Richard also had his supporters within the principality.

Richard's first victims were the Woodville family, whose power had grown during his brother's reign. The relatives of the dowager queen were systematically disposed of. Richard Grey, her twenty-five-year-old son from her first marriage, was executed at Pontefract for plotting against the new regent. Earl Rivers survived for another week, and was then beheaded. The 'protector' also turned on William, Lord Hastings, previously an ally, and had him executed for treason, apparently without trial. Hastings had a key role in Richard's strategy to retain political power, as he had been Edward IV's Lord Chamberlain and was guardian to the young king; this is why he needed to be removed. It has been speculated that he knew of the sinister plans for dealing with young Edward; once again, the evidence against Richard is circumstantial.

Richard was not content simply to act as regent for his nephew. He had quickly decided that it would be more efficient to rule in his own right. Revisionists claim that Richard's motives were of the best, and this may have been so. Whatever arguments the 'Ricardians' put forward, they cannot get around the fact that Richard deposed the nephew he had sworn to protect and took the throne for himself. He did so cleverly (or perhaps honestly, we will never know), accepting the word of a cleric who claimed to have married Edward IV to Lady Eleanor

Butler in secret, some time before the king took Elizabeth Woodville to wife. We know the identity of the priest only from the work of a French chronicler, Philippe de Commines, who names him as Robert Stillington, bishop of Bath and Wells.

If Stillington's story were true, it meant that Edward's sons by Elizabeth were illegitimate. There is some complexity in this statement, because a woman's child was deemed her husband's property, and a man could legitimize a bastard by acknowledging him or her, as long as it was his wife's child. In this case, however, it was the legality of Edward's marriage to Elizabeth that was called into question. The boys' illegitimacy, conveniently, made Richard himself the rightful heir to the throne. Just in case anyone suggested legitimizing them in retrospect, as a way round the problem, Richard added to the list of accusations one that seems to us quite outrageous. He allowed it to be suggested that, not only were his nephews illegitimate, but his brother, King Edward IV, had himself been a bastard.

The recently hyped theory of Edward IV's illegitimacy is based on various anomalies thought to have been observed in the records of his birth and baptism. Enthusiastic genealogists have claimed to have found the 'true' monarch of the UK (i.e. the direct descendant of the Duke of York's next son, George, Duke of Clarence), living a mundane existence in Australia. Clarence's descendants lost all rights to the succession when they were attainted by Edward IV.

Records of the period are sparse and one-sided, and it is not easy to be definite about how the government of the day came to the decision that Richard should become king in place of his nephew. Edward V was never crowned, and what happened to him after Richard stole his throne is not known. He was at first taken to the bishop's palace near St Paul's, then to the Tower of London, which at the time had a quite different reputation from the one it has nowadays. There was no reason for the prince to anticipate incarceration, and he was almost certainly lodged in comfortable apartments in what was then a royal palace.

Joining him there was the person closest to him – his little brother, Richard, Duke of York. Being the 'spare heir', Richard (known as 'Richard of Shrewsbury' after his birthplace) had been cosseted through childhood, receiving various titles and honours and even being married off, at the age of four, to an heiress who died not long afterwards, leaving him Duke of Norfolk. Being together must have been reassuring for the boys, which is probably why Elizabeth Woodville allowed herself to be coaxed into letting little Richard out of her care.

The case of the 'Princes in the Tower' is possibly the most famous historical mystery of all time, and unlikely ever to be solved. Most historians now believe that Richard had his two young nephews killed, in order to put an end to any comeback plans their supporters might have had. Some prefer to believe that the Duke of Buckingham ordered the killing, and others still theorize that the absent Henry Tudor, the House of Lancaster's claimant to Richard's throne, arranged the murder for reasons of his own. The balance of the evidence is clearly against Richard; those who argue otherwise lack an understanding of medieval power politics. For the sake of this narrative, we will keep an open mind.

It is almost certain that Edward V was dead by the beginning of 1484, when rumours to that effect were already circulating and Richard was doing nothing much to dispel them. If the boys had still been alive, the logical action would have been to ensure that they were seen in public. Instead, he issued an official statement that would have made any twenty-first-century prime minister proud. He simply denied the rumour, as he also, in the following year, denied rumours that he had murdered his wife and hoped to marry his niece.

In the circumstances, it is impossible to make any kind of judgement as to the character of King Edward V. Contemporary sources describe him in complimentary terms, but there is no way of verifying them. He goes down in history as one of the best kings we never had, but his career as Prince of Wales remains obscure.

Once again, there was an almost immediate replacement for Edward, Prince of Wales – in the form of yet another Edward, Prince of Wales. The new prince was the son of King Richard III and, by a fluke, was also the grandson of the late Earl of Warwick. Edward of Middleham remains a shadowy figure, overlooked by history perhaps because of the notoriety of his father combined with the mysterious fate of his predecessor as Prince of Wales.

We are not even certain of the date of his birth; we can only be sure that he was born some time between 1473 and 1476. He was his parents' only child. He takes the suffix 'of Middleham' because of his birthplace, Middleham Castle, which had been a possession of his grandfather, the Earl of Warwick. This became his parents' marital home while Richard III, still only a king's brother, held the position of Governor of the North.

The investiture of Edward of Middleham with the title of Prince of Wales took place in September 1483, at York Minster. An odd choice of location, one might think, but the north was Richard III's power base. With opponents of the new king already grumbling about the way he had seized the throne and speculating on the possible fate of his nephews, this would hardly have been the time to venture into the wilds of Wales. Furthermore, it sounds as though young Edward's health may have been in question, since he had been unable to attend his parents' coronation at Westminster Abbey a few months earlier. He had been officially created Prince of Wales at Pontefract during August.

The new king and queen entered the city in state. Records of large quantities of fabric and other decorations being ordered at short notice from the King's Wardrobe have led to speculation that the investiture ceremony was an afterthought, perhaps after the boy's parents had reassured themselves that he was up to the occasion. In the course of the investiture, young Edward was presented with the usual symbols of his new office: a gold coronet, a golden ring and a golden rod. After the event, the boy walked hand in hand with his mother in a state procession through the streets – an early royal walkabout. There was evidently no fear of crowd unrest.

Having taken possession of his new title, Edward of Middleham was returned to his Yorkshire home, while his parents went on tour, building up their personal popularity as insurance against the probability that a rival claimant would soon appear to threaten Richard III's hold on the kingdom. This happened sooner than might have been expected, when the Duke of Buckingham, previously Richard's staunch supporter, suddenly rebelled against his rule. It is often speculated either that Buckingham had just discovered the murder of the Princes in the Tower, or conversely that Buckingham himself had done the deed in the hope of currying favour with Richard and this had caused a falling-out. A third possibility is that Buckingham had never been interested in anything but furthering his own, rather feeble, claim to the throne. He was soon defeated, captured and executed as a traitor.

The letters patent by which Edward of Middleham was invested describe him as a boy of 'singular wit and endowments of nature'. These are meaningless compliments to a king's son, and we may assume that he was an average child. The fact that he was kept at home in the north, not paraded around the country or sent to Ludlow, speaks volumes. As an only child, all his parents' hopes and ambitions were vested in him, and one imagines he had every material possession that it fell within their power to offer. Perhaps Richard's love for his son is the real key to his despotic conduct. He wanted the throne, not for himself, but for Edward.

Whatever the truth, the new Prince of Wales lived for only another seven months. In April 1484, he was suddenly taken ill at his home in Middleham, and died before his parents could reach him. They were in Nottingham when the news arrived, and the Croyland Chronicle, a near-contemporary account, describes their grief in the most heart-rending terms. The boy was buried in the parish church at Sheriff Hutton, where his effigy may still be seen. There was a plan to establish a chantry chapel there, but it never came into being.

There was no replacement for this Prince of Wales. The queen, Anne Neville, died less than a year later, never having shown any sign of conceiving again. There was some talk of Richard remarrying, but it came to nothing. His heir was his other nephew, Edward, Earl of Warwick, who also happened to be Anne's nephew. As a child of the late Duke of Clarence, the boy was under an attainder as penalty for Clarence's treason, and it required some legal fiddling to make it possible for him to be replaced within the line of succession. Had Edward V still been living at this time, would it have been an option for Richard to name him as his heir, despite his alleged illegitimacy? It is noteworthy that, following Anne's death, the order of succession was changed yet again, reflecting Richard's preference for adult kings, and John de la Pole, Earl of Lincoln, was nominated as his heir.

As for Richard, he died in battle at Bosworth Field, and Henry Tudor, born in a Norman castle in west Wales, claimed the throne by right of conquest as King Henry VII. After Bosworth, Lincoln, albeit temporarily, renounced his claim on the throne in Henry's favour; two years later he would rebel against the new king, forfeiting his life at the Battle of Stoke Field.

Some may have felt that the death of Richard's only legitimate child, especially when followed by the death of his queen, was a judgement on the king for his conduct towards his nephews. It would be difficult, however, when considering the fates of Edward of Middleham's predecessors, to suggest that the ill luck that dogged his tenure of the title of Prince of Wales was in any way exceptional. The two Edwards who immediately preceded him had both died violently, and those princes who came before had hardly been notable for their longevity.

Might some have begun to believe that there was a curse on the title of Prince of Wales, particularly when borne by those with the forename 'Edward'? The Middle Ages were nearly at an end, but the pattern was far from being broken.

Arthur Tudor and
his More Famous Brother

Henry Tudor was a Welshman, and proud of it. The title of
'mab darogan' or 'son of prophecy', so enthusiastically claimed
by Owain Glyndŵr at the beginning of the fifteenth century,
was already being applied to the new King of England. Like
Glyndŵr, Tudor was descended from the royal house of Gwynedd.
It was said that, as a child, Henry, then Earl of Richmond, had
been presented to his half-uncle, King Henry VI, who had some
reputation as a man of piety and mysticism. According to this
fable, Henry VI had forewarned the future Henry VII that he
would one day sit on the English throne.

Henry Tudor was not, however, the saviour that some Welshmen had been hoping for. Although he brought peace and pros-
perity to a country that craved them, he did not elevate his
compatriots to important positions or honour Wales itself with
any kind of special status. He had, after all, spent most of his life
outside Wales. It was simple accident that he had been born in
Pembroke Castle, nearly three months after the death of his
father, Edmund Tudor, one of the half-brothers of King Henry
VI who were mentioned in previous chapters.

Although French royal blood (that of his grandmother,
Katherine of Valois) flowed in Henry Tudor's veins, his claim to
the English throne was actually through his mother, Margaret
Beaufort, who was descended in the illegitimate line from King
Edward III. The Beauforts were the result of John of Gaunt's
liaison with the famous Katherine Swynford. When, after the
death of his second wife, Gaunt married Katherine, the couple's
children were officially legitimized, but it was stipulated that
they could not inherit the throne. This is one of the reasons
why Henry Tudor claimed the throne 'by right of conquest'. As

Arthur Tudor, Prince of Wales, son of King Henry VII.
From a Victorian print.

king, he was one of the most successful in the history of Britain.

The Tudors were descended from Ednyfed Fychan, the seneschal or steward to Llywelyn Fawr. Through both his parents, Henry Tudor was also descended from Llywelyn himself. This mixture of Welsh and French blood may be the key to Henry's remarkable character; or it may have been to do with the ordeal he suffered as a small child, forced to flee the country after the deaths of his father and grandfather. Taken under the wing of his uncle, Jasper Tudor, he survived and was brought up in Brittany, where the people still use a variant of the Celtic language that is close enough to Welsh to be understood by Welsh speakers.

Henry does appear to have had a soft spot for Wales. He had adopted the red dragon, the standard of a Welsh prince, Cadwaladr, from whom he claimed descent. His naming of his first-born son is further evidence of where his loyalties lay. The name 'Arthur' had not been used for an heir to the throne since the original King Arthur to whose memory it represented a tribute. King Arthur, as all good Welshmen knew, had been Welsh, though later adopted by the English as a symbol of valour and independence; Arthur's people were the ancient Britons, the civilized Celts, driven from England by the Saxon hordes. Mallory and Tennyson had not yet given him the poetic trappings he enjoys today, and Arthur was perceived as a historical as well as a legendary figure. The name chosen by Henry underlined the justice of his own claim to be the 'son of prophecy'.

The new Prince of Wales was born on 20 September 1486, at Winchester, a city thought to be connected in some way with the activities of the original Arthur, but his investiture, at the age of three, took place at Westminster. It was, of course, unthinkable that it should take place in Wales. Wales at that time had no real cities, even though it had cathedrals. The population of Carmarthen, the biggest town, was only around 2,000, whereas the population of Bristol was in the region of 10,000 and of London perhaps as much as 90,000. The people of Wales were largely engaged in subsistence farming, and were often as isolated from one another as they were from the English. Realistically, there was nowhere in Wales that an elaborate ceremony could have been held, nor was the transport network up to the task.

Like his namesake, Arthur was borne down the Thames to his investiture on a royal barge. To support the image of the new prince as a returning hero, Henry wasted no time in preparing his son for the kingship that was to follow. Arthur would receive the best education as well as being trained to become the warrior his father had never been. The book-learning part of the plan proceeded well; the fighting held less appeal for the boy, who was undersized and one of nature's introverts. Henry's younger son, who came along a couple of years later, was a more promising specimen, and perhaps benefited from the greater freedom afforded to a son who was *not* his father's heir. He was, of course, the prince we now remember as King Henry VIII.

To return to Arthur, there had been many worse prospects for the throne. Arthur was about ten when his father, perhaps wishing to toughen him up as well as to begin his training as a monarch, sent him off to Ludlow to take his place as head of the Council of Wales and the Marches. This body, the very same set up by King Edward IV, was still functioning (as it would continue to do until 1689), and had by now established its role in the government of Wales. Henry VII saw its chairmanship as a suitable beginning for a king in waiting. He surely never connected the disastrous fate that had befallen young King Edward V, on his way home from Ludlow, with the future fortunes of his own son. Believing himself, not the late Owain Glyndŵr, to be the true son of destiny, it never occurred to him that he could be affected by any 'curse'.

Arthur Tudor's council consisted mainly of Englishmen, his father's most trusted advisers, and it provided the Welsh with a focus for their allegiance. The Welsh nobility, in the form of families like the Griffiths, Vaughans and Herberts, crossed the border to seek favours from Arthur, though the prince was not expected to return the compliment by visiting them at home, or indeed to enter Wales at all.

How did Arthur spend his time at Ludlow? He certainly studied, his father having sent tutors along with him, and a governor, Sir Reginald Bray, to oversee the household. We know that he learned Latin, the language of the law and officialdom, because he used it to write to his bride-to-be. He must, like his predecessor Edward V, have spent some time at Tickenhill, in Bewdley, Worcestershire, for it was there that his proxy marriage to the Spanish princess, Katherine of Aragon, took place in 1499. Katherine was the youngest daughter of Ferdinand and Isabella and a sister of the Infanta who had once been held in reserve for King Edward V.

The real royal wedding, in November 1501, was carried out with great ceremony, and was followed by feasting, jousting (in which the heir to the throne did not participate) and dancing. It looked like the beginning of a brilliant career for the future king. He had survived childhood, that most dangerous of times, and looked ready to begin a family of his own. Back to Ludlow he went with his new bride. The couple were only fifteen, but in 1501 that was considered adulthood – Henry VII's own mother had been only thirteen when she gave birth to him.

Within months, Katherine was a widow. A plague, or fever, had struck Ludlow, and both the prince and princess had fallen victim to it. Katherine returned to the land of the living to find that her husband was dead. The fever was put down to the generally unhealthy climate of the Welsh borders. Never again would Henry VII trust his son to that environment. When, a year later, he bestowed the title of Prince of Wales on his younger son, there was no question of the future Henry VIII being sent to Ludlow. He stayed at Westminster, where his parents could keep an eye on him. The Tudors' grasp on the kingdom was not so strong that they could afford to lose their spare heir.

Most people, even if they know nothing else about the history of Britain, are aware that Henry VIII married Katherine of Aragon, and that he later divorced her in favour of Anne Boleyn. Fewer people understand the technical justification for the divorce action, which turned on the question of whether Katherine remained a virgin after her brief cohabitation with Arthur. Papal dispensations, for those who could afford them, were easy to come by. As long before as the thirteenth century, Edward I had asked the Pope for a general dispensation in order to marry off his children to others of suitable birth. As most of the European royal families were related, most of their marriages were illegal according to strict Catholic teaching. The dispensation granted to enable Henry and Katherine to marry had been given, nominally, on the understanding that Katherine and Arthur had not been intimate during the four months of their marriage. At this distance in time, it is difficult to assess the arguments for and against them having been so.

In favour of the royal couple having had sex is the fact that they were both fifteen, an age at which society regarded them as adults; we might be tempted to believe that they were even more likely to have given in to their natural instincts than today's typical fifteen-year-old. On the other hand, they were *not* typical fifteen-year-olds. Katherine had been brought up strictly in the Catholic faith. She is hardly likely to have gone into a frenzy of lust on seeing the weakling she had married, and might well have wanted to delay the inevitable for as long as possible. Arthur himself had been brought up in an isolated fashion, and, being a less than magnificent physical specimen, might well have felt unready to do his husbandly duty.

Our impression that Katherine told the truth about the survival of her virginity is inspired by the knowledge that she was a pious Catholic who believed that perjury was a mortal sin. It is, however, worth noting that her personal confessor was among those who believed the marriage *had* been consummated. Looking at it more pragmatically, we see that she had no choice but to proclaim herself a virgin in order to obtain the Pope's permission to marry Arthur's brother – without this prospect, she could look forward to an ignominious return to Spain, or perhaps to life in a convent. Having lied, if that is what she did, she would have felt obliged to maintain the lie rather than risk losing her own status and, more importantly, sacrificing the legitimacy and consequent status of her daughter, Mary.

All in all, it remains a knotty problem, and the need to solve it is non-existent, with the Reformation nearly five hundred years in the past. Religion and marriage would both continue to play an important role in the lives of the princes of Wales for centuries to come. To return to Henry VIII, he held the title of Prince of Wales for six years, from 1503 until his accession to the throne in 1509. For the whole of this period, he was officially betrothed to Katherine of Aragon. Had it not been for this, he might not have been invested as Prince of Wales quite so quickly; there was perceived to be some inconsistency in his continuing as mere Duke of York when his wife-to-be was already Princess of Wales. Consequently, Henry was invested with the new title less than a year after his brother's death. As

Arthur's widow and princess dowager, Katherine expected to receive a portion of the revenues of Wales, just as Joan of Kent had done, but her father-in-law declined to pay these. It is more than likely that Henry Tudor was also responsible for his son's tardiness in bringing Katherine to the altar; Henry VIII married her almost the moment he came to the throne.

Like his late brother, Henry, when Prince of Wales, was given his own household, but at Westminster, not Ludlow. He was given the same level of education, but he spent more time with his father than Arthur had done. It is as though Henry VII could hardly bear to let his surviving son out of his sight. On his deathbed in 1509, the king is said to have expressed a wish that his son should marry Katherine immediately. Perhaps, in a flash of insight, he realized it was not a good thing for a king, however young, to be without an heir.

That Henry VIII had a strong awareness of Wales and its potential is suggested by his action, as king, in bringing about the union with England. The Act of Union of 1536 brought long-awaited stability to the principality, confirming its status as an integral part of England. From a modern point of view, it may be considered to have been both a good and a bad thing for the Welsh as a people. They had a legal identity, and could plead their cases in a proper court. On the other hand, they were obliged to do so in English, which for most was not their first language and for many was as foreign as the French or Italian tongues.

Under the terms of the 1536 legislation, Henry VIII took back the independence of various Marcher lords and created new counties out of their former territories. By a strange paradox, it was as a result of the new set-up that Wales actually came into being as a political and territorial entity recognized by law. As for the Prince of Wales, he no longer had a role in the government of Wales, only the right to a share in its Crown estates and revenues. It made no difference to Henry; he had already relinquished the title, and did not yet have a son on whom to bestow it.

One of the reasons for the introduction of the Act of Union may have been the rebellion of Sir Rhys ap Gruffydd in 1531, a signal that the Welsh had still not entirely settled down to English rule. The new law also provided for the Welsh to have

Henry VIII, created Prince of Wales after the death of his brother Arthur but better known for his six wives. From a Victorian print.

representation in Parliament. The second Act of Union, in 1543, established the Welsh system of court circuits, leaving Monmouthshire in a limbo from which it has never quite emerged. The passing of these acts put an end to any suggestion that the Prince of Wales was responsible for administering Wales on behalf of the king.

Perhaps surprisingly, Henry VIII never bestowed the title of Prince of Wales on his own much-prized son, the future Edward VI. This may have been because the Acts of Union had made a significant change to the status of Wales, and it may have been considered that the title was redundant. Could this have been an excuse? Was it that by now Henry too believed that the title carried ill luck and wanted to protect his only legitimate male heir? If this was the case, it did not work. Edward ruled England for only six years, dying at the age of fifteen, quite probably from a sexually transmitted disease passed to him by his father at conception.

Henry Stuart and his More Infamous Brother (and Nephew)

A hundred years on, the curse of the Princes of Wales had not yet been defeated. The next to hold the title was a promising youth of sixteen. The Tudor dynasty had come and gone, leaving its mark but no permanence. All three of Henry VIII's children had ruled in turn, with varying degrees of success, and now all were dead and England was forced to look outside its borders for a ruler who carried the same blood. The best on offer was King James VI of Scotland, a great-grandson of Henry VII. James had certain advantages to offer, not least the fact that he had been brought up a Protestant.

By the time he added the English throne to his Scottish one, James was already married with two sons. The elder, Henry Stuart, was a fine young man, whose promise was widely proclaimed. The younger son, Charles Stuart, was a weakling, who suffered from a speech impediment and was painfully shy. He is thought to have suffered from rickets as a child. He would later have the dubious distinction of being the shortest adult male ever to rule the country.

Prince Henry had been born at Stirling, in 1594, the first child of James and his wife, Anne of Denmark. (Anne had been chosen specifically to reinforce the official Protestant religion of her husband's kingdom, but she later became a closet Catholic.) Despite having signed the death warrant of his grandmother, Mary, Queen of Scots, only seven years earlier, Queen Elizabeth I of England stood godmother to the young prince. He was named in honour of Elizabeth's father, Henry VIII, the king who had brought Protestantism to England. In infancy, Prince Henry was taken from the bosom of his family and placed in the household of the Earl of Mar, much against his mother's

Henry Stuart, Prince of Wales.
From a Victorian print.

wishes. It gave the boy the opportunity to be influenced by someone other than his eccentric father, and he became a staunch adherent of the Protestant religion, whereas James still wavered. Henry did not return to the family fold until 1603, when his parents were setting off for England. By that time, Mar had grown so used to having him around that the king had to issue a warrant to get him back; the queen was so upset that her seventh pregnancy ended in a stillbirth.

Henry was already attracting his own group of political followers by the time he was invested as Prince of Wales in June 1610, a full seven years after his father took the throne. He was at the centre of a circle of talented youths, including the young Earls of Essex and Southampton, Lord Harington, and the Cecil boys, grandsons of Elizabeth I's chief adviser, Lord Burghley. There were many who disapproved of King James's growing willingness to be ruled by favourites, and looked forward to Henry's reign, linking their own ambitions to it. The investiture ceremony took place at Whitehall, before both Houses of Parliament and many other dignitaries. The proceedings are recorded in detail, and, like his predecessors, the new prince was given a sword, a ring and a rod of gold. At the revels which accompanied it, Henry's young brother Charles appeared in a masque as Zephyr, wearing green satin and silver wings. By this time, he had lost some of his early awkwardness, and the audience was charmed.

The indications are that Henry himself had initiated his father's decision to create him Prince of Wales, having looked into the matter and felt that he was missing out. He had, after all been Duke of Cornwall and Duke of Rothesay since his father ascended the throne in 1603, but King James appears to have overlooked the normal practice of giving his heir the title to the principality. This is hardly surprising, since there had not been a Prince of Wales since Henry VIII gave up the title in 1509, and it had slipped out of the collective memory. The new heir apparent employed a researcher to dig up the history of the title, and satisfied himself that it should indeed be his by right, along with any income appertaining to it.

Even if it was Henry's idea, it makes sense that James should have gone along with it. Before he took the English throne, he had written two treatises on the theme of kingship. In *The Trew*

Law of Free Monarchies (published in 1598) he equated kings with gods, in that they 'sit upon God his throne in earth and have the count of their administration to give unto him'. In these terms, the Prince of Wales would represent a kind of lesser god, reporting upwards to his father.

For the English and Welsh, having a Prince of Wales again would be a novelty. For the Stuarts, the title was a completely new one. The dukedom of Rothesay, which came with Henry, was the traditional one for the heir to the Scottish throne, vested in him by the Scottish Parliament in the fifteenth century. Combining it with those titles normally held by the heir to the English throne was symbolic of the union between England and Scotland brought about by the merger of their monarchies. Rothesay and his other Scottish titles, which Henry held from birth, have also been inherited by the heir apparent right down to the present day.

Duke of Rothesay is not, however, a title that bears direct comparison with Prince of Wales. The dukedom first passed to the Scottish Crown in 1398, when it was held by David Stewart, and the Scottish Parliament confirmed it as an official title of the heir apparent in 1469. Along with it go the Earldom of Carrick, the Barony of Renfrew, and the title of Lord of the Isles, forfeited to the Scottish Crown under King James III of Scotland in 1475. Unlike the Duchy of Cornwall, that of Rothesay has no property associated with it. Nevertheless, by the time he turned sixteen, the new prince had an annual income of nearly £50,000 a year, an amount whose value in today's terms we can scarcely imagine. Instead of blowing the lot on loose women and fast living, as one might have expected, he used much of it to sponsor the arts in Britain, recruiting Italian and Huguenot craftsmen to work on public buildings and theatrical displays. Among the properties he owned was the manor of Kennington, at one time the home of the Black Prince. The defunct former palace was replaced with a grand new house.

Stories about Henry Stuart are numerous and almost entirely complimentary. Perhaps we should take with a pinch of salt the recollections written down following his death, just two years after his investiture. We know that he excelled at sport, and was well educated, but these things in themselves do not necessarily make a good king. Nevertheless, it is clear that he was talented and popular. He was actively involved in the theatre, to the extent that he organized a piece of theatre entitled *Prince Henry's Barriers*, with speeches by Ben Jonson and scenery designed by Inigo Jones, for his own amusement. He enjoyed jousting and hunting, and his investiture was celebrated with a tournament and a water pageant, the latter starring the noted Elizabethan actor, Richard Burbage. Henry was very different from his father. It is generally acknowledged that his death was a tragedy, not just for his family, but for the kingdom. We see it in this perspective mainly because of the poor performance of his successor as Prince of Wales.

At the time of his death, Henry was eighteen, an age at which many princes were already married. (We may recall that Richard of Shrewsbury, the younger brother of King Edward V, was already a widower at the age of ten.) Many candidates for his hand had been paraded before Henry, but he had not seen anything, either Protestant or Catholic, that appealed. The only hint of a romance in his life was his relationship with Frances Howard, the wife of his friend the Earl of Essex. Frances was already notorious, and would later be involved in a scandalous divorce followed by a murder case. An affair with her would at least be evidence that Henry was human, but negotiations for his eventual marriage with a suitable princess were stagnating at the time of his death. The most likely candidate looked like the six-year-old Christine, a daughter of the late Henri IV of France and Marie de' Medici. King James was favouring a Catholic alliance as a means of reinforcing his policy of religious tolerance.

History is full of might-have-beens, but it is almost certain that the English Civil War would not have happened if either Henry Stuart or his heirs had survived. That having been said, Henry was certainly of a more warlike disposition than either his father or his brother. Perhaps because he was in better physical shape than James, he had a fascination with military science, and was an early war-games player, using scale models of artillery and armoury to acquaint himself with techniques and tactics. He had his own network of agents overseas, who kept him informed of the latest developments in international politics. He was widely seen as the future protector of Protestant interests in Europe.

Henry never came to Wales. Even his father did not do so until 1617, well after the prince's death. The prince knew about his antecedents, though, and it is not fanciful to suppose that his Scottish origins may have helped him to understand the position of the Welsh within his future kingdom. It may be unrealistic to imagine that he would have attempted to do anything about it, had he lived to be king, but he certainly associated with Welshmen. One of his major interests was in things maritime, and he was a patron of Thomas Button, the Welsh sea captain who sought the North-West Passage as early as 1612. His court 'surveyor', meanwhile, was the Welsh-descended architect and designer, Inigo Jones.

It was becoming almost traditional for the heir to the throne, once possessed of the title of Prince of Wales, to die and leave his position to a son or younger brother. It had happened to the Plantagenets, with the Black Prince, and to the Tudors with Arthur, and now it happened to the Stuarts. Henry was carried off by typhoid in November 1612, before anyone had time to think seriously about the consequences, having succumbed to a fever after eating raw oysters and swimming in the river Thames. As soon as the dust had settled, James I of England confirmed his younger son, Charles, as his heir. His investiture as Prince of Wales, however, did not come for another four years.

Charles may not have been the most promising Prince of Wales in England's history, but no one could have predicted what a catastrophe his reign would be for the country. As a prince, he did the usual things. He looked around for a bride (not finding one until after he ascended the throne) and embarked on alliances that would continue into later life. Under his father's influence, he had become a firm advocate of the doctrine of the divine right of kings. This would be his undoing.

Like his elder brother, Charles had been born before his father acquired the English throne, at Dunfermline on 19 November 1600. When Henry was created Prince of Wales, Charles became Duke of York. The two boys, six years apart in age, had separate households, and although Charles clearly worshipped his elder brother, it was from afar. He was not old enough to benefit directly from Henry's influence. Henry was naturally closer to his sister, Elizabeth, who was nearer his age. She became Queen of Bohemia (the 'Winter Queen') and would one day supply her native land with much-needed Protestant heirs.

One thing the princes had in common was that both behaved with greater dignity than their father. Both were, however, strong-willed. Henry, even as a youth, had opinions of his own. Charles, on the other hand, inherited many of his father's. The *Basilikon Doron* had been written by James as an instruction book on kingship for use by his sons. In 1604 it was translated into the Welsh language, in recognition of the advent of a new dynasty whose attention needed to be attracted to the existence of the small country attached to the left-hand side of England. With Henry gone, the contents of the book proved equally relevant to Charles.

After Henry's death, there was no shortage of less suitable role models available to the new Prince of Wales at his father's court. One such early influence was the Duke of Buckingham, George Villiers. Buckingham was James I's favourite of the time, a handsome, amoral creature who quickly exerted the same magnetism on the teenage Charles as he had on Charles's father. As a child, Charles had not shown the appropriate respect for 'Steenie' (the nickname James used for Buckingham). As a young man, he came to adore him.

The investiture of Charles as Prince of Wales took place in November 1616, just before his sixteenth birthday. The ceremony was held at Whitehall, almost on the spot where he would meet his death thirty-two years later. Enough time had passed since his brother's death for public enthusiasm for a celebration to have been rekindled, and the festivities, though less lavish than those for Henry's investiture, were nevertheless impressive. The queen refused to attend because she could not bear the memories of Henry that came with the occasion, but Charles received all the same honours as his brother had done, including the coronet. There were great celebrations in Ludlow, still the seat of the Council of Wales.

Charles resembled his brother in his love of the arts. Eighteen months after his investiture, he appeared in Ben Jonson's masque, *Vision of Delight*. His career as heir to the throne was long enough for him to become used to the adulation and following that it brought him, and this must have helped to turn his head. Buckingham took him to Spain, in search of a marriage alliance. It was planned that the prince would travel incognito, with the assistance of one Endymion Porter, a

Spanish-speaking courtier. The ship in which he travelled was commanded by a Welshman, Thomas Herbert, but it was a poorly planned expedition. The overland journey to Madrid was more perilous than either Charles or his father can have anticipated, and Spanish officials were horrified when the two young men revealed themselves.

They spent six months in the country, where Charles was fully exposed to the mysteries of Roman Catholicism. He confessed to feeling overawed by the brilliance of the Spanish court, with the 'manie jewels' worn by those who frequented it. During his stay, he had his portrait painted by the great Velazquez. The young prince was enjoying a privilege that had never been granted to his late brother Henry: the opportunity to broaden his mind with overseas travel. He drank in the sight of Segovia Cathedral, the palace of Philip II and the old masters on display at Valladolid.

Between them, however, Charles and 'Steenie' managed to make a mess of things. The Spanish were outraged by Buckingham's behaviour (the Spanish ambassador to Britain even proposed the earl's execution), and all Charles's attempts to come face to face with the Infanta were foiled. One of the prince's Welsh companions, Sir Sackville Trevor, had to save him from drowning in Cadiz harbour. Moreover, the demands made on behalf of the prospective bride were excessive, and could not possibly be met. James began to worry about the extended absence of the Prince of Wales, writing (in what seems to us a peculiarly modern style): 'Never look to see your old Dad again . . . if ye see him not before winter.' Charles returned in November, an occasion so joyful it had to be recorded in a painting by the Dutchman Cornelis Vroom. For a time, the prince was extremely popular in the country for having failed to bring home a Spanish bride. Catholicism was still seen as a threat by the majority of the British population.

During his European travels Charles had, however, met the girl who would later become his wife. Henrietta Maria was the youngest child of King Henri IV of France by his second wife, Marie de' Medici, and thus a sister of the bride who had been proposed for Henry Stuart. Although brought up a Catholic, her credentials may have seemed preferable to those of a Spanish princess. It was well known that her father had given up his

Protestant religion only to secure the throne of France (declaring that 'Paris is worth a Mass'). The marriage negotiations with France began early in 1624, but the princess did not arrive until after the death of King James I. She turned out to be as confirmed a Catholic as any Spaniard could have been, and would actually refuse to participate in her own coronation ceremony because of its religious significance.

The catalogue of incompetence represented by the Spanish trip would be characteristic of Charles's reign as king. The prince was not, however, a hopeless case. He had seen the difficulties encountered by his father in dealing with Parliament. He developed some experience of government through being obliged to act as virtual regent for the last few months of his father's life. Like his late brother, Charles was well educated, and his sensitivity and even his prudishness may have endeared him to many of those who were repelled by his father.

Although he was highly intelligent, James's manners and appearance were gross, and by the end of his reign he had become a figure of fun. The recognition of this must have affected Charles, either by making him want to emphasize his kingly dignity in order to distance himself from his subjects and avoid ridicule, or perhaps by making him go out of his way not to fall into the same habits as his father. The famous triple portrait of him, created in 1636 by Sir Anthony van Dyck, has been dubbed 'the epitome of royal aloofness'. Whatever his intentions, Charles failed to capture the imagination of the nation. They had tolerated James because there was no alternative; now, they were beginning to wonder if there *was* an alternative after all.

Almost as soon as he came to the throne, Charles began to make an enemy of Parliament. James had died in debt. In order to stage a magnificent funeral, Charles borrowed more. Wars with France and Spain, an outbreak of plague in London, plus the sour aftertaste of the marriage treaty, combined to make Parliament stingy with money. When, in 1627, the favourite, Buckingham, ignominiously failed to relieve La Rochelle, he was impeached. The king's response was to dissolve Parliament. In the process of launching another expedition, Buckingham was murdered, leaving Charles without his greatest friend. Parliament had called the duke the 'great author of our misfortunes', but

*Charles Stuart, Prince of Wales after the death of his brother Henry,
and later King Charles I. From a Victorian print.*

his loss made it difficult for Charles to function. Unable to come
to terms, Charles I shut down the 1629 Parliament and did not
call another for eleven years.

In 1633, the king decided to return to the land of his birth for
a second coronation at the cathedral of St Giles in Edinburgh.
The separate Scottish parliament was at first more amenable to
his wishes than the English one, and Charles was able to introduce a new prayer book, the intention being to bring the two
countries' modes of worship closer together within the Anglican

rite. When the Scottish clergy attempted to use the prayer book for the first time, one Sunday in 1637, a street trader called Jenny Geddes threw her stool at the dean of Edinburgh and started a riot. Naturally, the king refused to withdraw the prayer book, and thus began the Bishops' Wars. A royal army marched on Berwick-on-Tweed, but a peaceful solution seemed to have been reached when Charles (now advised by the unpopular Thomas Wentworth, Earl of Strafford), agreed to give the Scottish Parliament the final say. He could not have anticipated that they would abolish the supremacy of the bishops.

Charles's other kingdom, Ireland, was still predominantly Roman Catholic and hence willing to support his actions against the renegade Presbyterian Scots. It was not enough. The collection of 'ship money' had already caused a campaign of widespread civil disobedience in England, and there was now nothing for it but to recall the English Parliament. Once again the king showed his lack of political foresight. Instead of responding to his call for action against the Scots, Parliament took away his power as an absolute monarch, and refused to be dissolved. In the meantime, the Irish Rebellion of 1641 resulted in the massacre of thousands of Protestant settlers. Instead of the Irish sending an army to suppress the Scots, it was the other way around, and years of savage subjugation followed, which are at the root of the twentieth century's Irish troubles.

Strafford, along with the Archbishop of Canterbury, William Laud, was accused of treason by Parliament. Charles sacrificed his most loyal lieutenant in the hope of preserving his own power. Strafford, on hearing that his death warrant had been signed, warned his listeners, 'Put not your trust in princes.' The king, still reeling from the loss of another valued counsellor, made another huge strategic error at the beginning of 1642, when he attempted to arrest five Members of Parliament, Pym, Hampden, Holles, Haselrig and Strode. Having failed, he was left with little option but to launch a military campaign. His one remaining hope, the Nineteen Propositions sent him by Parliament in a last-ditch attempt to avoid war, he rejected, emphasizing his determination to remain in control with the words *Nolumus leges Angliae mutari* ('We do not consent that the laws of England be changed'). In the course of the next seven years, Charles I would lose two civil wars, be imprisoned, escape, be imprisoned again and finally be tried and executed by the Parliament he had so scorned. To his last breath, he rejected any suggestion that he was subject to their jurisdiction. In his speech from the scaffold, he declared: 'I go from a corruptible to an incorruptible Crown.'

Charles had expected solid support from his former principality of Wales. Llancaiach Fawr, a manor house in Gwent, was one of the places he visited in 1645 to drum up support for his cause, and it is preserved as a museum of living history, where servants welcome tourists in the idiom of the day, wearing contemporary costume. The owner of the house, Colonel Edward Prichard, was known by Charles to be wavering in his allegiance to the Crown – hence the social visit. The colonel was more than willing to welcome the king to dinner and offer him a bed for the night, but turned his coat almost as soon as Charles was out of the house and went over to Cromwell.

Such was the political unrest of the time that the investiture of Charles I's eldest son, the future Charles II, as Prince of Wales, never took place. It was taken for granted, from his earliest youth, that the title would be his, and he was called Prince of Wales almost from the moment of his birth on 29 May 1630, at St James's Palace. However, when, in 1638, he received the Order of the Garter, it was as 'Prince of Great Britain', Duke of Cornwall and Duke of Rothesay. Records suggest that he officially donned the more prestigious title some time early in the English Civil War or just before it. This would make sense at a time when his father was struggling to stabilize the monarchy's position in the country, and would explain why no elaborate investiture ceremony was possible.

It was suggested by the Welsh Renaissance scholar, Dr John Davies, rector of Mallwyd, that it would be a good idea for the prince to learn the Welsh language, which was far from dying out despite the best efforts of previous monarchs. Dr Davies proposed, in the preface to his *Dictionarium duplex* of 1632, which he dedicated to the Prince of Wales, that the prince 'be imbued from the cradle . . . with the ancient language of this island, which is now restricted to your own Welsh people'. Implicit in these words was Wales's innate superiority over England in terms of a continuous historical tradition. 'Knowing languages', Dr Davies argued, 'is no indignity for princes.'

Bilingualism, then as now, was a skill more widespread among the Welsh than the English.

The Prince of Wales took an active part in the war his father had started. In 1645, at the age of fifteen, he was sent to Bristol by King Charles to take command of the Royalists in the west of England. In reality, he was there as a figurehead, and did no fighting. He had held the post for a matter of months when the Royalists were defeated at Naseby, forcing the prince and his entourage to flee Bristol. The king wrote to his heir to tell him to leave the country, and in March 1646, he set sail for the Scilly Isles, just off the coast of Cornwall. From there, the little royal party moved on to Jersey, where the prince's charming manners made him many friends.

Charles junior was a much better prospect as Prince of Wales than his father had ever been. Six feet tall and swarthily handsome, he attracted women like moths around a flame. Soon he joined his mother in France, at the court of the youthful King Louis XIV. The daughter of the Duc d'Orléans was earmarked as a wife for him, but she spurned the suit in favour of more prosperous candidates for her hand. Charles was unable to speak to her in French, and the prospect of a marriage faltered. Having quickly realized the benefits of his physical attractiveness, he seems to have been unconcerned that a royal alliance was not forthcoming.

Throughout the civil war, the Prince of Wales represented the best hopes of the Royalist cause. Even when his father had thrown away the throne and his own life, his heir was far from giving up the succession. In the opinion of the Scots, he had become king immediately his father was executed in January 1649, but when, in 1650, he arrived in Scotland, it was to be greeted with a general lack of enthusiasm. The main reason, of course, was his failure to meet the dominant religious criteria. On his arrival he hastily accepted the 'Solemn League and Covenant', a document which insisted on the Scottish Kirk remaining independent of the Anglican Church, and which had previously been rejected by King Charles I. The Presbyterians now ran the country, and would only allow those of moral character to remain in the army, the result being that they met with a crushing defeat against Cromwell's troops at the Battle of Dunbar. Charles II, meanwhile, was almost as much a prisoner in Scotland as his father had been in England, even after his coronation as King of Scotland at Scone on New Year's Day, 1651.

Later that same year, at the Battle of Worcester, he failed to win back the crown of England, and famously evaded capture by hiding in an oak tree. His daring escape after the battle was possible only because he retained a loyal following among ordinary subjects – people like Jane Lane, the colonel's daughter who risked everything to transport him to the southern coast, disguised as her manservant, 'Will Jackson'. We may surmise that Charles's good looks and personal magnetism had a lot to do with his popularity, but he was undoubtedly intelligent and shrewd, becoming more so as he grew older and his interest in the opposite sex gradually ceased to be the driving force in his life. In the meantime, he was obliged to wait patiently in France for the inevitable. After Oliver Cromwell's 'reign' as Lord Protector, the kingdom was left in the hands of his surviving son, Richard Cromwell, a peace-loving youth with no political inclinations, who quickly handed over control of the government and acquiesced when the restoration of the monarchy was proposed.

At Breda in Holland, Charles had set up a temporary court, and it was there that General Monck sent emissaries to offer him his father's throne back. The ship on which he sailed home had been called the *Naseby*. Now it was renamed the *Royal Charles*. Welcomed at Dover by Monck, Charles progressed to London, where a parade was held and the Puritan mindset that had controlled the kingdom for the last ten years was banished as ordinary people rushed to witness the lavish celebrations. By coincidence, it was King Charles II's thirtieth birthday, and with him was the most notorious of his mistresses, Barbara Palmer, better known to us by her maiden name of Barbara Villiers. Such was her hold over the king that she ended up a duchess in her own right. Charles would acknowledge all her illegitimate children, even one popularly believed to have been fathered by the young soldier, John Churchill, later Duke of Marlborough.

During his period of exile in France and Holland, Charles had entered into an unwise liaison with Lucy Walter, the daughter of minor Pembrokeshire nobility. Lucy gave birth to a son, James, whose father was probably the prince (though this is far from certain, given her history). The boy, born in the year Charles I was executed, was brought up by Lord Crofts on the new king's behalf, and used his surname. Following the Restoration, he was acknowledged by Charles II (along with several other royal bastards) and given the title of Duke of Monmouth. In due course, Monmouth became a rallying-point for those who were dissatisfied with Charles on account of his Catholic leanings, and even more so with his younger brother, James, Duke of York, who had been well and truly indoctrinated by his mother into her faith. Lucy Walter having been a good Protestant, her meretricious lifestyle was overlooked and the story went about that she had been secretly married to the Prince of Wales.

Under the circumstances, it might have suited Charles II to legitimize Monmouth. Despite having sixteen acknowledged bastards by at least seven different women, he had no living children by his legal wife, Catherine of Braganza. As his reign drew to a close, he must have foreseen the chaos that would ensue when his brother succeeded to the throne, and yet he refused to make Monmouth his heir. It seems likely that this was because there had been no secret marriage to Lucy Walter, and Charles, whatever his other faults, was not dishonest enough to invent one. It is generally accepted that he died a committed Catholic, but he never allowed his subjects to see him practise the faith.

As king, his reign, like his father's, was fraught with religious and political difficulty. Despite having promised an amnesty to those who had sentenced Charles I to death, the new king had many of them brutally executed. Oliver Cromwell's body was dug up, hung in chains and ceremonially beheaded. Charles II was as determined a ruler as his father had been, but chose his battles with greater care. The British people were not yet ready to go through another revolution; consequently the king's in-discretions were gladly overlooked, and the 'Merrie Monarch', as he came to be called, maintained his popularity for the best part of twenty-five years.

During the early years of his reign, he was advised by Edward Hyde, Earl of Clarendon, whose daughter Anne had married Charles's younger brother, James, during their continental exile.

The future King Charles II with his brothers and sisters.
From a Victorian print.

Clarendon had been faithful to the prince throughout his
wilderness years, but, following a disastrous war against Holland,
he was impeached and forced into exile. He was supplanted by
the 'Cabal', an advisory council so named because of the
initials of its members – Clifford, Arlington, Buckingham (the
son of 'Steenie', whom Charles's father had so adored), Ashley
and Lauderdale.

Secretly paid off by his kinsman, Louis XIV, Charles opted
out of the war against France, and turned his attention to
problems at home. Having tried and failed to introduce a policy
of religious toleration, he was eventually obliged by Parliament
to dismiss some of his closest advisers on the grounds that
they represented a threat to national security. Much the same
was said of his faithful queen, Catherine, herself a Portuguese
Catholic. So steadfast was Charles in his defence of her that
she wrote to her brother: 'Every day he shows more clearly his
purpose and goodwill towards me, and thus baffles the hate of
my enemies . . .' Furthermore, he succeeded in blocking the

Exclusion Act which would have prevented his Catholic brother from succeeding him.

King Charles II, taking a leaf out of his father's book, ruled without Parliament for the last five years of his reign. The one thing the 'Merrie Monarch' had not counted on was his own death, which came at the most inopportune moment. A few years earlier and the memory of civil war might have made James II less reckless. A few years later and the birth of James's son might have been welcomed by the nation. As it was, Charles died of a stroke, aged only fifty-four, and left the country with an enormous void, to be filled by a most unworthy man.

The Pretenders

It is somewhat ironic that James Edward Stuart should have gone down in history as 'The Old Pretender', since his official tenure of the title of Prince of Wales lasted only until he was six months old.

James was the 'warming-pan baby' of the public scandal. So desperate were the Catholic King James II and his second wife, Mary of Modena, for a son that in August 1687 James went on a pilgrimage to Holywell in Flintshire to pray for one. It seems to have done the trick, but the public never quite trusted their king and queen. When the child was born, they were alleged to have smuggled an impostor into the birthing chamber by means of a warming-pan. To anyone who has seen a warming-pan, it is a baffling idea, but, as usual with history, no one can say for certain that there was no exchange.

James II was a hugely unpopular king, in the same league as his father, King Charles I. Like Charles, James believed in his divine right to rule. Whereas Charles merely had Catholic sympathies, his younger son had been brought up in the Catholic faith by his mother, Queen Henrietta Maria, and had affirmed his position in the course of the reign of his elder brother, the pragmatic Charles II who had kept his own religious beliefs secret. James II, if not quite a fanatic, was prepared to go to considerable lengths to maintain the rights of his fellow Catholics. This made him so many enemies that it was almost inevitable his reign would end as it did, in a revolution. Known as the Glorious Revolution because it was accomplished with minimal bloodshed (at least on the British mainland), it ended with James being exiled to France, while his Protestant daughter, Mary, and Mary's Protestant husband, William of Orange, ruled in his stead.

James Francis Edward Stuart, Prince of Wales (the 'Old Pretender'), with his son, Charles Stuart, styled Prince of Wales (the 'Young Chevalier'). From a Victorian print.

James II's son was styled Prince of Wales from birth, and held the Earldom of Chester and the Duchies of Cornwall and Rothesay to go with it. When he was only six months old, his father fled the country, taking the heir to the throne with him. As William of Orange advanced towards London, the prince was taken first to Portsmouth, where Lord Dartmouth refused to take him on board a ship of the fleet, and then back to London, where the safety of the baby and his mother was entrusted to a French exile, the Duc de Lauzun. Lauzun accompanied them to Gravesend, where the Catholic William Herbert, Marquess of Powis, awaited them with appropriate transport. Powis, the descendant of medieval Marcher lords, would remain a loyal Jacobite, living out the rest of his life in exile.

After William and Mary both died childless, Mary's younger sister, Anne, took her turn on the throne. Like Mary, she left no surviving children, and once again the country needed to look outside for its next ruler. There were two obvious candidates. The Protestant claimant was Sophia Dorothea, Electress of Hanover, a granddaughter of James I through his daughter, Elizabeth. She was an elderly woman, and died six weeks before Queen Anne, leaving her son, George, as Elector of Hanover and heir to Anne's throne. His accession was not, however, a foregone conclusion.

James II never gave up hope of regaining his throne, even after his resounding defeat of 1690 at the Battle of the Boyne in Ireland, at the hands of his son-in-law William III. James's supporters were known as 'Jacobites' (from 'Jacobus', the Latin for 'James'). He died in exile in France in 1701, leaving his heir, James Stuart, still known to Stuart adherents as Prince of Wales, as the rightful king in the eyes of Catholics everywhere. The pretender was by all accounts an attractive young man. If the timing had been right, things might have gone very differently for him. Unfortunately for James, his strategy for winning back the throne of his ancestors was wrecked by personal misfortune.

The Prince of Wales was brought up at the French court, where King Louis XIV had taken it upon himself to protect the 'rightful' royal family for reasons that were more political than religious. Louis had ostentatiously welcomed Mary of Modena and her son in person, the moment he heard of their arrival in France. It was a gesture of chivalry likened by the historian

Macaulay to the honour shown by the Black Prince towards the late King John of Bohemia. Their home was to be the fourteenth-century château of Saint-Germain-en-Laye, where James's mother later gave birth to another healthy child, a daughter named Louisa.

At Saint-Germain, only a short distance from Louis XIV's magnificent palace of Versailles, an alternative royal court quickly grew up as the deposed king arrived to join his family. Louis granted them a generous pension, still in the hope or expectation that a Catholic monarchy would one day be restored to the British Isles. The prince was brought up in his parents' religion, and was paraded through Paris to take his first communion, a symbolic gesture as well as a ceremonial occasion. At this time there still remained some hope of his being officially recognized as heir to the throne of Great Britain. Following the death of his father, in September 1701, the former Prince of Wales was immediately recognized by the French, and was proclaimed King James III of England and VIII of Scotland, but he would remain a stranger to his kingdom, apart from a single visit in 1715.

It was not until 1702, some months after his father's death, that James was attainted by an Act of Parliament, making certain that he could not claim his throne by right of inheritance. There had been no rival Prince of Wales in the interim, and it was the accession of Queen Anne to the throne vacated by her childless sister and brother-in-law that gave Parliament the impetus it needed to consider the problem of the Protestant succession. They were right to be concerned. Anne came to the throne at the age of thirty-seven, but her last pregnancy had been two years earlier. Of her eighteen children, none had survived childhood. William, Duke of Gloucester, the last of James II's grandchildren, had died in July 1700, at the age of eleven.

Anne became queen six months after the death of James II in France, when the would-be James III was only thirteen, and he chose not to challenge his half-sister directly. When Anne's husband, George of Denmark, died in 1708, the already remote prospect of another Protestant heir was lost. The Scots had lost their separate Parliament in 1707, and neither they nor the rest of the population had any real affection for the House of Hanover, whose succession had been decreed by Parliament.

The Electress Sophia, daughter of the 'Winter Queen', had a certain reputation, but her son George was uninspiring, and had not even learned to speak English as his mother did. The time was ripe for rebellion.

In 1708, six months before Queen Anne was widowed, the twenty-year-old James attempted to sail into the Firth of Forth with thirty troop-loaded French ships, counting on the Scots to support him once he landed. Detained in France by illness (probably measles), he showed some strength of character in writing to his mother, Mary of Modena, that 'the body is very feeble, but the spirit is so strong it will bear up'. By the time he set sail, the English were expecting him. It was Admiral George Byng (not to be confused with John Byng, his son, executed in 1757 for dereliction of duty) who drove off the French fleet, forcing them to return to mainland Europe via the north of Scotland. James's pleas to be allowed to land at Wemyss Castle were ignored by his minders.

In the following year, he improved on his military experience by serving in the French army at the Battles of Oudenarde, where the Duke of Marlborough took advantage of the French military's internal quarrels, and Malplaquet, where Marlborough once again triumphed, despite losing over a fifth of his army.

It is worth noting that James could have been recognized as Anne's successor if he had been willing to renounce his Catholic faith. Anne herself was believed to be prejudiced in his favour; he was, after all, her little brother. Relying heavily as he did on the patronage of King Louis XIV, he could hardly have been expected to make that decision in advance of Anne's death unless he left France, which had become his home. It was only after her death in 1714 that the Jacobites once again considered a serious assault on the now 'United' Kingdom. John Erskine, sixth Earl of Mar, having lost his position in government under the new king, George I, renewed his Jacobite sympathies and raised the clans in support of King James III and VIII. With the help of supporters in northern England, the Jacobites began to march south. Not until Preston did they meet any real opposition, and then they suffered not only defeat, but desertion and the loss of a substantial part of their total fighting force.

The ''15' became another of those lost opportunities that could have changed the course of British history significantly.

James did not arrive in Scotland until just before Christmas, by which time the Jacobites had met the English in battle again, the insurgency was effectively over and it was too late to rally further support. The Battle of Sheriffmuir, in November 1715, was indecisive though it was claimed as a victory by 'Bobbing John' (as Mar was nicknamed), and the rebellion quickly fizzled out.

Although plans were being made for his coronation at Scone, the traditional crowning-place of the Scottish kings, James, on seeing the meagre size of the welcoming party, recognized that all was lost. Having failed to win over more support, possibly on account of his reserved manner, he departed in February 1716. William Maxwell, fifth Earl of Nithsdale, one of the Jacobite leaders captured at Preston, was due to be executed in the Tower that very month. His countess (the former Winifred Herbert, daughter of the loyal Welshman who had taken the baby James out of the country in 1688) arranged a daring escape, and the pair followed their 'king' to Rome, where they spent the rest of their lives.

James is another of those characters neglected by history, in his case because of the much more colourful impression left by his son. It is worth pausing to consider what we know of the Old Pretender's personality. In 1715, he was a man of twenty-seven and had acquired an 'unimpassioned and stately' presence which failed to suggest a man of action. Thirty years later, his son would do a little better.

The pretender's return to France in 1716 without his crown was, of course, not welcomed by the French. Louis XIV was dead, and the country was ruled by regents who would have preferred not to see the pretender again. He ended up living in Rome, under the protection of the Pope, and did not marry until 1719, when he was united with Maria Casimire Clementina, daughter of a Polish prince and a Catholic like himself. They had two sons. The younger, Henry, became a Roman Catholic priest and eventually a cardinal, ensuring that he could never produce potential heirs. It is therefore with the elder brother only that history tends to concern itself.

'Bonnie Prince Charlie', as he is universally known, was styled Prince of Wales from birth, and it was as nominal Prince of Wales that he arrived in Scotland (officially joined with England in 1707 by his aunt Anne), to attempt to reclaim his father's kingdom for the Stuart dynasty. He had even less military experience than his father; he had been present at the siege of Gaeta at the age of fourteen, and that was about it. Baptized with the grand name of Charles Edward Louis John Philip Casimir Sylvester Maria, this young man had become the last great hope of the Jacobite cause.

There was no special feeling for Wales in his heart. Born in Rome, Charlie had been brought up outside his grandfather's kingdom, and it was only through the loyalty of the Highland Scots that he could hope to obtain the foothold he needed to snatch back the throne. When he landed on the isle of Eriskay in 1745, having lost several ships to the English en route, he was recommended by the local nobility to 'go home'. Charles is supposed to have replied: 'I am come home.' If he did say it, he did so in the thickest of foreign accents. Nevertheless, the Highland leaders, having had thirty years to think about it, were persuaded to accept him and to raise his father's standard. His attempt to retrieve the throne for the Stuarts came close to succeeding, the Jacobite army occupying Edinburgh and beginning the march on London, turning back only at Derby. Communications were not good enough for the prince to learn that his distant cousin, George II, was preparing to abandon the country.

Ironically, it was his chief advisers, overruling the prince's natural inclinations, who made the disastrous decision to return to Scotland. Even after their retreat, there were military gains, but several weeks were wasted in attempting to recapture Stirling Castle, and in the meantime the Duke of Cumberland, George II's favoured younger son, arrived in Aberdeen with another army. There followed the catastrophic defeat at Culloden, whose repercussions were felt in the Scottish Highlands for many decades afterwards.

For Charlie, however, the only thing that now mattered was escape. He wrote to the Highland chiefs, explaining why he was leaving Scotland. He could no longer be of any use there, he said, but 'by my going into France instantly, however dangerous it be, I will certainly engage the French court either to assist us effectually and powerfully, or at least to procure you such terms as you would not obtain otherwise'. No doubt he had some idea of living 'to fight another day', but that day would never come. He took a boat to the Hebrides, landing first in Benbecula, then at Stornoway on the island of Lewis.

The story of how the prince fled from one place to another, always with the assistance of loyal Jacobites, is well known. Best known of all is his legendary journey, dressed as a woman ('Betty Burke'), in the company of twenty-four-year-old Flora MacDonald, a native of South Uist. Flora was imprisoned for her part in the episode, but her name has been revered ever since as the epitome of female courage and constancy. Even Charlie's rival as Prince of Wales admired her, and recommended his wife, the Princess of Wales, to take her as an example. According to legend, when Flora's body was buried on the isle of Skye, it was wrapped in the bed-sheet Charlie had used.

In September 1746, after nearly six months on the run, the 'young Chevalier' arrived safely back in France. The promises of French military support came to nothing, and the prince spent most of the next twenty years living in Avignon, a papal state where he had been forced to move under the terms of the Treaty of Aix-la-Chapelle which ended the War of the Austrian Succession. Two years later, the thirty-year-old prince paid a secret visit to London to participate in a Jacobite plot. William King, to whom he was introduced, admired his looks but commented that 'in a polite company he would not pass for a genteel man', adding that he appeared ungrateful and insolent. The prince allegedly carried around a copy of the Book of Common Prayer, in order to convince Protestants that he had converted to their faith. The plot never got off the ground.

The health of his father, the 'King over the water', meanwhile, was declining. James continued to play the king in a modest way, claiming that there was 'no greater Englishman' than himself. For the last two years of his life, he was confined to his bedroom, and it was there, on the first day of the year 1766, that he died peacefully. His body lay in state for three days in an Italian church, receiving the respects of the local nobility and British exiles, and he was buried with some ceremony in St Peter's basilica.

Charles was living an increasingly debauched existence. To the few remaining loyal Jacobites, he was now King Charles, but there was nothing of the dignity of kingship in his lifestyle. Even Pope Clement XIII declined to recognize him as

King of Great Britain. The 'Count of Albany', as he was generally known, eventually married, in 1772, a woman who had been born seven years after the failed Jacobite rebellion. The main reason the French monarchy had procured Princess Louisa of Stolberg-Gedern as a wife for him was in order that the Stuart line should not die out. Louisa failed to provide him with an heir, however, and we cannot help suspecting that this was as much his fault as hers.

In 1770, a visitor described Charles as 'bloated and red in the face' from heavy drinking, though still showing traces of his youthful good looks. We can imagine what the young princess must have thought when she saw her bridegroom-to-be. It is easy to understand how, especially after the beatings he is said to have given her, she was tempted into a liaison with the Italian writer, Vittorio Alfieri, with whom she went to live at Baden after the Pope granted her permission to separate from her husband.

Charles was left alone, and decided to relocate from Florence to Rome. His only child was illegitimate, a daughter born in 1753 – the year after his wife – to a mistress, Clementina Wilkinshaw. (Like Louisa, Clementina had deserted the prince because of the brutal treatment she received at his hands.) Charles brought this young woman, Charlotte, to live with him, and had her legitimized. Since becoming an outcast from the European courts, he had been known as the Count of Albany, and now he created his daughter 'Her Royal Highness' the Duchess of Albany (the style and title were of course not recognized by the British crown).

The Jacobite 'king' suffered a stroke in January 1788, and died on the last day of the month. Like his father, he was buried at St Peter's in Rome. That is not quite the end of the story. Charlotte had several illegitimate children, and through her, Charles is reputed to have descendants who are alive today, but the contemporary records are obscure. Following the death of Charles's younger brother, 'King Henry IX', in 1807, the three Stuart claimants were commemorated in St Peter's by the erection of a magnificent marble monument, designed by the most famous sculptor of the day, Antonio Canova. Among those who paid for it was the official Prince of Wales, the future George IV, who could afford to be generous now that the biggest threat to the Hanoverian succession had been eliminated.

For those who continue to support the Stuart claim on the throne of the United Kingdom, including a good proportion of Scots, 'Bonnie' Prince Charlie, however undeserving, was King Charles III. This is possibly the basis for the unsubstantiated rumours that the present Prince of Wales has decided, if he ever takes the throne, to do so as King George VII.

Dapper George and Poor Fred

Up until the Hanoverian dynasty, only seven of the thirteen 'official' Princes of Wales had gone on to become king. The record would improve over the next century, but not without a hiccup.

It began well enough. In 1714, when he arrived in Britain, King George I's eldest son was not only an adult but a married man with sons of his own. His wife, Caroline of Ansbach, was attractive, cultured and clever, which was just as well, because the new Prince of Wales had none of these qualities. He was nevertheless a 'safe pair of hands' into which the throne of Great Britain might pass at some future date. As such, the British public welcomed him. An Act of Parliament granted him the revenues of the principality of Wales, a privilege that would not be passed on to his descendants.

Things might have gone very well if the prince's father had shared the people's good opinion of him. However, there was a history between them. When George I was still merely Elector of Hanover, his wife, Sophia Dorothea of Celle, after an unsuccessful attempt to elope with Count von Königsmark, had been cast off and locked up in the Castle of Ahlden for the rest of her life. Her two children were taken from her to be brought up at court, and young George never saw his mother again. Despite her undoubted guilt, it was a cause of considerable ill will between the two Georges, and continued to be so until the death of King George I. Possibly the father may even have suspected that his son was a bastard, foisted on him by his erring wife; but he could hardly disown his only male heir. The prince, who once tried to swim the castle moat in order to get to his mother, always looked forward to releasing her from captivity, but she died seven months before his father.

George, the first Hanoverian Prince of Wales, later King George II.
From a Victorian print.

Here began the Hanoverian tradition of family antagonism. George II hated his father, and the feeling was reciprocated. After the old man's death, so it is said, the new queen, Caroline of Ansbach, was looking through some private papers when she discovered that a scheme had been hatched to pack her husband off to the American colonies. Despite this ill feeling, however, George junior had been created Prince of Wales almost the moment his father arrived in Britain, by the usual method of 'letters patent' but apparently with no great ceremony. Although the records state that he was given the usual regalia, including a 'cap', they do not describe the ritual. It may be inferred that the Hanoverians had a limited understanding of the procedure. Against the background of family discord, it suggests a desire to 'fit in', adopting the traditions of their new, united, kingdom rather than comprehending its complex history.

The public falling-out of George I and his heir began in 1717, with the christening of a new grandchild, the young Prince George. The king had invited the Duke of Newcastle to be god-father. The Prince of Wales disliked Newcastle on principle, and attempted to eject him from the proceedings. In response, George I booted his own son out of his residence in St James's Palace. The Prince and Princess of Wales were obliged to find alternative lodgings, and virtually set up a rival court at their new home in Leicester Square. Those who could not obtain political preferment from the king attempted to build an alliance with the heir apparent.

So it continued for the rest of George I's reign, so much so that, when the old king dropped dead during one of his periodic visits to Hanover (which he still ruled), the Prince of Wales could hardly believe his luck. George and Caroline were roused from sleep, in their country home at Richmond, by the prime minister, Sir Robert Walpole – with whom Caroline had had the foresight to make friends. Walpole brought the news that they were now king and queen. George's immediate reaction was to call Walpole a liar.

Walpole was telling the truth, however, and the wheel soon came full circle.

Before leaving Hanover, George II and his wife had four children. The eldest, Frederick Lewis, born on 20 January 1707, was his father's heir, and as such was in line to rule Hanover. At this stage, the throne of Great Britain was only a dim and distant possibility. Frederick's grandfather decided that the boy should be educated according to his known destiny, and turned him into a kind of deputy, allowing the infant to take the place of honour at certain state occasions. When the Elector was chosen as King of Great Britain, he had little choice but to leave Hanover for England, and his son went with him. The new Prince and Princess of Wales took with them all their children apart from Frederick. The little boy, now aged seven, was left behind to act as a figurehead for the royal family.

It was a strange upbringing, even by the standards of British royalty. Hardly any wonder that, when Frederick eventually arrived in London, in 1728, eighteen months after his father's accession to the British throne, the new Prince of Wales was a stranger, not only to his people, but to his own family. Nevertheless, within a month he was invested with the titles of Prince of Wales and Earl of Chester. It was not his first exposure to traditional British, or Welsh, royal titles. The title of Baron Snowdon, given him by his grandfather in 1726, was one that had been used by the princes of Gwynedd prior to the Norman conquest of Wales in the thirteenth century.

Frederick seems to have been a man of many contradictions. His manners were, by British standards, uncouth to the point of grossness; yet he is acknowledged to have had an appreciation of the finer things in life that his father lacked. Music and the arts were particular interests of his, and he would in time take pride both in his home and in his wife and children. It is not quite clear at what point his parents began to resent him. It is most likely that they did not look forward to his joining them in Britain, for he had been given privileges by his grandfather that must have seemed the rightful prerogative of his father. Moreover, he had taken the step of attempting to marry without their permission.

The lucky young lady on whom Frederick's eye had fallen was Princess Wilhelmina, the daughter of Friedrich Wilhelm I of Prussia. Wilhelmina was his first cousin, the daughter of George II's only sister, and she had been selected for Frederick by his grandfather. When the time came, however, George II scuppered the plans. He was not prepared to be upstaged by the arrival of a married son. Wilhelmina was married off to another prince, and Frederick was forced to remain a bachelor, on the income deemed appropriate for a bachelor. He did not give up the search for a wife when he arrived in Britain. The elderly Duchess of Marlborough had an appealing grand-daughter, Lady Diana Spencer, and began secret negotiations with the prince. This time the unofficial wedding plans were discovered by Robert Walpole, and the Prince of Wales seemed doomed to remain unmarried.

Historians' sympathies tend to lie with Frederick, and no wonder. Left alone in Hanover, isolated and undisciplined, his better qualities might well have been subsumed by his baser instincts. Neither his father nor his grandfather provided much of a moral example. Both had many mistresses, not necessarily selected for their good looks or gracious manners. Despite the outwardly successful marriage of the future George II to Caroline of Ansbach, he continued to look elsewhere for romantic enter-tainment. The most publicly acknowledged of his mistresses was Amalia Sophia, Countess von Walmoden, who had come over with the royal family from Hanover. She was created Countess of Yarmouth by her lover, who lacked even the excuse that his father, George I, had, of not having a wife available. Frederick had fallen into the same habits, and would continue in that vein.

There is a story that the prince's seal once had to be retrieved from the hands of a prostitute. Apocryphal as this may be, we know that Frederick had at least one mistress. Ann Vane was the daughter of Gilbert Vane, Baron Barnard, and had been the mistress of Lord Hervey, who befriended the prince in the early days of his career as Prince of Wales. It has been suggested that the son she bore, FitzFrederick Vane, was in fact not fathered by the prince at all, but by Hervey. In this as in so many other cases, things might have turned out very differently if paternity tests had been available earlier in history. As it was, Frederick was devastated when both Miss Vane and her son died in 1736. It may have been this bereavement that finally persuaded him to give up debauchery for good; or it may have been that all he wanted, right from the beginning, was to settle down with the right woman and produce legitimate children. After all, it was only his parents' prevarication that had prevented him from doing so several years earlier.

Frederick, Prince of Wales, son of King George II.
From a Victorian print.

Frederick had additional motives. His parents were refusing him the revenues from Wales, to which he felt entitled, whilst showering money on his favoured younger brother, William, whose apartments at Hampton Court were built and decorated at a cost of over £3,000. At approximately the same time, Frederick employed the same designer, William Kent, to build him a royal barge, fit for a Prince of Wales to travel in. In attempting to maintain this lifestyle, he incurred massive debts. There was no shortage of friends prepared to advance funds to the future king, who had been promised £100,000 a year from Parliament but was getting only half that sum from his father. One such acquaintance was the disgustingly wealthy George Bubb Dodington, who lent Frederick the necessary deposit for the purchase of Carlton House, which would become the prince's married home.

The girl eventually chosen as Frederick's bride, Augusta of Saxe-Gotha, was not quite seventeen and had no experience to speak of, in any department. She was neither beautiful nor clever, but she was at least modest and her character beyond reproach. An observer described her as having 'sweetness of countenance, mixed with innocence, cheerfulness and sense'. From the moment she arrived in Britain, Frederick set out to impress her, regardless of the fact that it was unquestionably a marriage of convenience. This was not by any means a necessary approach, and we warm to him when we picture him taking the teenage princess for a boat trip down the Thames in his magnificent barge, treating her to dinner and the opera. He was certainly starting off on the right foot.

Whether their marriage ever grew into an equal relationship is doubtful. Unlike her mother-in-law, the feisty Caroline, Augusta seems to have been content to let her husband wear the trousers, and obeyed him when he instructed her to do everything she could to annoy his parents. When their first child was due to be born, the queen (who had, perhaps as a result of Hervey's resentful gossip, developed a firm belief that her son was incapable of fathering a child) insisted on being present at the birth. This was like a red rag to the Prince of Wales, who could hardly bear to go along with anything his parents wished. While they played cards in one of Hampton Court Palace's great state apartments, Frederick hurried his wife down the back stairs and out to a waiting coach. Her waters had broken, and he knew the birth was imminent, but he ignored her pleas to be left where she was, and the coach headed for St James's Palace, about twelve miles away.

Accompanying Frederick and Augusta was Lady Archibald Hamilton, an older woman believed by many to be the prince's mistress. If the stories were true, it was nothing unusual for a royal mistress to be an integral part of the royal household. Two of Augusta's ladies of the bedchamber were also rumoured to be mistresses of the Prince of Wales at various times.

The following day, when the king and queen discovered how their son had deceived them, they were suitably furious and determined to withdraw any remaining privileges. The new-born child was a girl, and they had nothing much to lose by ignoring her existence. Six weeks later, Frederick and his family were evicted from their apartments at St James's Palace and had to find alternative accommodation very quickly. There was no shortage of well-wishers prepared to assist a future king. When it was falsely reported that the king, on his way back from a trip to Hanover, had been lost at sea, the mob was almost ready to crown Frederick.

By the time a male heir arrived, Queen Caroline was dead, and George II made no serious attempt to bond with his new grandson. Despite subsequent events, they would never become close. When Frederick attempted to visit his dying mother, his father's response was brutally frank: 'Bid him go about his business for his poor mother is not in a condition to see him act his false, whining, cringing tricks now.' For good measure, he added: 'Bid him trouble me with no more messages, but get out of my house.'

The queen, before her death, had cultivated Robert Walpole, who finally retired from office in 1742. He had been the cornerstone of George II's government, and the king would find it hard to survive political life without him. In the following year, George became the last British king to lead his own troops into battle, against the French at Dettingen. Frederick, much to his disgust, was always kept away from the military, perhaps because his father feared his general popularity would turn to armed uprising. There was enough of that to contend with, the Jacobites being so active. George recognized the threat from his Stuart cousins, whereas Frederick, deprived of a place at the head of the army by his younger brother, merely had a cake made in the shape of Carlisle Castle to mark its fall to the rebels, as an amusement for his dinner guests.

Frederick's long-awaited son, Prince George William Frederick, was born at Norfolk House, 31 St James's Square, in June 1738. His parents had been forced to move into this town house after being thrown out of St James's, and they soon acquired a country home, Cliveden, where they spent increasing amounts of time. Their last five children were born at Leicester House, the London residence formerly used by George and Caroline, and it was there that the prince's life would come to an end.

Frederick's hobbies were mostly related to the fine arts, something his father had never much appreciated. (George II once famously remarked that he hated all poets and painters.) The

Prince of Wales's patronage went to artists such as the Venetian
Jacopo Amigoni and the Frenchman Jean–Baptiste Vanloo, both
of whom painted portraits of the prince and his household.
The French engraver Joseph Goupy and the English painter
John Wootton also benefited. As shown in the famous portrait by
Philippe Mercier, Frederick played the cello, and he was a patron
of the Italian opera composer Nicola Porpora, who brought the
castrato Farinelli to sing in Britain at the prince's behest. The
eminent poet Alexander Pope was another of those who enjoyed
royal hospitality.

Like so many princes before him, Frederick fell at the final
hurdle. He was forty-four when he died, and the exact manner
of his death is disputed. It began with a sporting accident, when
he was struck by either a tennis or a cricket ball (depending
which version you believe). The result was an abscess, which
burst – or it may have been an abscess on the lung. (George Bubb
Dodington, in his diary, says that the post mortem demanded
by the king revealed an abscess 'in his side'.) Alternatively, we
read, he died of pleurisy, or maybe pneumonia. In other words,
no one seems quite sure. Dodington blames the prince's phys-
icians for not recognizing the significance of the 'black thrush'
which was one of his symptoms. Frederick's death was just as
much of a shock to Dodington as to everyone else. Just a few
hours before, the prince had been sitting up in bed, receiving
visitors, drinking tea and eating bread and butter, until seized
with a fatal fit of coughing and 'spitting'.

Frederick was mourned by many, including his wife and
children, but not by his father. Queen Caroline had predeceased
him by nearly fourteen years, allegedly proclaiming on her
deathbed that her one consolation was that she would 'never
see that monster again'. Mother and son would be buried just
yards apart in Westminster Abbey.

George II paid lip service to the loss of his heir. Although he
did not attend the funeral, he did send his condolences to the
widow, and soon afterwards bestowed the title of Prince of
Wales on his young grandson, the future George III. Augusta,
expecting her ninth child at the time she lost her husband,
affected gratitude for the king's attention, whilst planning her
revenge. The old man carried on, taking less interest in politics
than he had done when his son was around to oppose him,

but never quite losing his interest in the opposite sex.

The epitaph written for the Prince of Wales by an anonymous wit with Jacobite leanings is generally regarded as summing up Frederick's unsuccessful career:

> Here lies poor Fred,
> Who was alive and is dead.
> Had it been his father,
> I had much rather.
> Had it been his sister
> Nobody would have missed her.
> Had it been his brother,
> Still better than another.
> Had it been the whole generation,
> So much better for the nation.
> But since 'tis only Fred
> Who was alive and is dead,
> There is no more to be said!

This seems far from fitting, when one considers that 'poor Fred' was one of the most active and high-profile Princes of Wales in history, and popular for much of his lifetime. Some would argue that it was this very unwillingness to take a back seat that made him as many enemies as friends. It seems even sadder that Frederick's own parents had no feelings for him; he was barely cold in his grave when his successor, his twelve-year-old son, was invested with the title vacated by his death.

Mad King George and the Regency

History has been unfair to King George III. In many ways he was the best of the Hanoverian kings, as well as being the longest-reigning. He came to the throne at the age of twenty-two, and lived to be eighty-one. He was a lover and patron of the arts *and* sciences, was considerate towards his wife and many children, and had higher moral standards than any of the other Georges. Unlike any of his predecessors as Prince of Wales, he had a good relationship with his father.

The fact that George III spent long periods of his reign unable to rule because he was debilitated by mental illness has coloured the modern view of him (particularly the opinions of the American colonists and their descendants). We tend to think of him as someone who spent hours tied to a chair or sedated, who spoke to trees and often did not recognize his own family. Yet, for the first twenty years of his reign and more, he was perfectly normal – at least, by royal standards – and took his regal duties very seriously indeed.

It is with George III as Prince of Wales that we are mostly concerned here, and he held the title for about nine years, from the death of his father in 1751 to his accession in 1760. During these years, George relied on his mother for emotional support, and Augusta of Saxe-Gotha felt obliged to maintain her independence of the royal family in order to hang on to her son's affection. She had not been used to thinking for herself, and her husband, Frederick, Prince of Wales, seems to have believed her incapable of so doing. All she could do was to insist on keeping her son close to her, rejecting on his behalf the offers made by his grandfather, George II, of a prodigal income and a household of his own. Up to a point, Augusta's

GEORGE Prince of WALES.

George, Prince of Wales, later King George III.
From a Victorian print.

strategy worked: when she died of throat cancer in 1772, her eldest son was at her bedside, having visited her faithfully, at least twice a week, since becoming king.

Contemporary observers claimed that both Frederick and Augusta were over-critical of their eldest son, and that this tendency became worse in Augusta after her husband's death, when she realized that George's reign would begin sooner than previously thought. Frederick had left nothing to chance; his will gave strict instructions to his son and heir on how to conduct himself in future. From his father, George inherited a love of the arts and music, once telling the novelist Fanny

Burney (whose father was a renowned musician) that he found the inability to appreciate music as inexplicable as an inability to talk. The prince was not, however, given the opportunities for foreign travel that might have broadened his mind still further.

Various tutors were appointed by the king to handle the education of the new Prince of Wales and his younger brothers. The only one Augusta was really happy with was John Stuart, Earl of Bute, an ambitious politician who offered support to the mother as a way of getting nearer to the son. Their close relationship became a source of scandal, a delight to the gutter press, who lampooned the Dowager Princess of Wales mercilessly for the rest of her life. Bute, like his late friend Frederick, Prince of Wales, was a great patron of the arts, and encouraged his pupil's interest in activities such as architecture, horse-riding, books, art collecting, clock-making and wood-turning.

The stories about how the adolescent prince was treated are doubtless exaggerated, many of them coming from the political opponents of his parents. His cloistered upbringing had, how-ever, affected his view of life, making him very different from the preceding Hanoverian kings: less vulgar in his manner, for one thing, and more concerned with the welfare of his subjects than either of the first two Georges had appeared to be. Only much later would he lose his grip on reality. His account of his mother's death, as written to one of his absent brothers, closely resembles that of a twenty-first-century man: 'We had the melancholy scene of knowing she could not last, but that it must not be taken notice of as she did not choose to think so,' he wrote, after his last deathbed visit. George was still only thirty-three when his mother died.

As a boy, George III was taught to love his closest family, but to hate and fear more distant relatives, such as his Uncle William, the notorious Duke of Cumberland, scourge of the Jacobites. While Cumberland was showing his nephew round his private apartments, the boy took an interest in a sword he saw hanging on the wall. When Cumberland brought it down to show him, however, the terrified George shied away, thinking harm was intended. This was clearly not a healthy frame of mind for him to be in. On 25 October 1760, when the prince was twenty-two, his grandfather died of a heart attack while sitting on the toilet, and the young man had to conquer any remaining fears.

The question of his marriage had arisen before he came to the throne, his grandfather having spotted a young lady who appealed to his own undiminished preferences. George II had enough sense left to realize that he could hardly marry the teenage Princess Sophia Caroline of Brunswick-Wolfenbuttel himself, and proposed her as a bride for his grandson. Interference from the prince's mother put a stop to that. Once the Prince of Wales was king, however, it became imperative that he should marry and father an heir. There is a much-publicized story that he married Hannah Lightfoot, a Quaker girl. If it is true, and if Hannah was still living in 1761 when he entered the Chapel Royal for his wedding to Princess Charlotte of Mecklenburg-Strelitz, then his marriage was bigamous and his heirs illegitimate, even if he had no children by Hannah. If, as seems to be the case, Hannah was already dead, there was no encumbrance.

George III's own preference is said to have been for Lady Sarah Lennox, one of the famous Lennox sisters, who were illegitimately descended from King Charles II. The young king confessed to a friend that he thought about Lady Sarah all the time. A marriage within the British nobility, however, was as undesirable as it had been for his predecessors, and Lady Sarah was related to the Fox political dynasty. George did as he was advised, and married the German princess selected for him.

Away from his mother's domineering presence, the young king now gradually exerted his independence. Charlotte turned out to be a supportive and suitable marriage partner, docile, pliable and devoted to her husband and children. Seventeen at the time of her marriage, she was easily moulded, and adopted her husband's wide-ranging interests. The couple were patrons of Gainsborough, Zoffany, Ramsay and Benjamin West, among others. They commissioned and collected silver, porcelain, ceramics and furniture. George III may have lost the American colonies, but North America was not immune to his cultural influence.

Their family life was happy, at least in the early years. In adulthood, their sons would turn out rakes and playboys, almost incapable of fathering a legitimate heir between them, whilst their daughters, discouraged from marrying, would fulfil themselves in secret liaisons and, in one case, a bastard child. Many years later, when the next Prince of Wales fell out with his wife, his younger brother (later William IV), commented that, 'He has married a very foolish and disagreeable person, but he should have made the best of a bad bargain as our father has done.' This sheds a somewhat different light on George III's marriage, and more probably reflects what William himself felt about his mother than what the king felt.

Buckingham House (now Palace) had been built in 1703 for John Sheffield, Duke of Buckingham, and looked very different from the building we see today. It was bought by George III for his new queen in 1761, and shortly afterwards work began on its refurbishment, supervised by William Chambers, the Scottish architect who had been one of George's tutors. It gradually became the principal royal residence in London.

On 12 August 1762, the king was told his wife had given birth to a daughter, but said he did not mind it being a girl, as long as she was healthy. The Earl of Huntingdon had been too hasty in bringing the news, for the baby was a boy. For several days, the new prince was put on display to selected visitors. He had already been named Prince of Wales, even before he was christened George Augustus Frederick. His father was nothing if not respectful of British royal tradition.

Within the next ten years, a further seven royal children were born. George III became a family man, as his father had been, though for different reasons. The family took over Kew Palace, a Jacobean residence originally known as the Dutch House. In his early childhood, the young prince's development and education made astonishing strides. He was making short speeches at the age of two, and could read and write well by the time he turned five. His first official tutor, the Earl of Holdernesse, took charge of the Prince of Wales and his younger brother, Frederick, Duke of York, and kept them apart from other children, just as George III's mother, Augusta, had done with her sons. Eventually the princes began to rebel against both the strict educational regime and the coddling to which they were subjected. Holdernesse was replaced by a new team, which included the Bishop of Lichfield, Richard Hurd. Hurd produced a written programme of study for the boys, including literature, music and sport, so that in his teens Prince George was considered a model youth, and had a much easier manner than his father had done at the same age.

George III recognized inherent weaknesses in his eldest son's character, and was determined to correct them. Although he loved his children, the king's approach to their upbringing was not subtle. The Duke of York advised his brother the Prince of Wales earnestly to stay on good terms with their father, and to 'do everything which you can to keep well with him'. Two of the king's own brothers, the Duke of Gloucester and the Duke of Cumberland, had made secret and unsuitable marriages, and this was the motivation behind the passing of the Royal Marriages Act of 1772. Under the terms of this legislation, no member of the royal family could marry without the king's consent. It might have been anticipated that the Prince of Wales would be the first one to fall foul of this new law.

In 1780, when the Prince of Wales turned eighteen, his father set out some ground rules for his future lifestyle. For example, the king wrote: 'Whenever you are desirous of dancing, I shall very readily forward it – but I shall not permit going to Balls and Assemblies at private houses.' Relations between them did not improve. The Prince of Wales wrote to his younger brother: 'I think his behaviour is so excessively unkind that there are moments when I can hardly ever put up with it.' Things were even worse between George and his mother, Queen Charlotte. As he told his brother: 'She accused me of various high crimes and misdemeanours and which I answered and in the vulgar English phrase gave her as good as she brought.' One of the king's major complaints against the Prince of Wales was his rudeness to his mother. Here we recognize shades of his grandfather, Frederick, and the poor relationship that prince had with his mother, Queen Caroline.

In 1783, with tongue firmly in cheek, the king bemoaned the political dilemmas with which he was beset, and suggested that it might be better for him to leave the country and hand over the reins of government to his son, who, never having been able to understand politics, would not have the same problems. By 1784, the prince's debts amounted to nearly a million pounds in today's values. Prince George then threw himself on his father's mercy, pleading for them to be paid.

In the meantime, he became friendly with the Whig leader, Charles James Fox, a relationship which caused great consternation to the king, who had been blamed by the Whigs for the loss of the American colonies. Fox was a great gambler, and led the prince further astray, if such a feat were possible. When the prince came of age, Fox stood up for him in his attempt to obtain an allowance of £100,000 per annum, which the king wanted to halve, saying, 'I have little reason to approve of any part of his conduct for the last three years'.

In an effort to placate him, the prince was given Carlton House, a town residence (no longer standing) near the present-day Trafalgar Square, acquired by his grandparents when they were out of favour with George II. In 1783, the prince moved in and commissioned extensive alterations, which were bound to stretch the public purse still further. Later that same year, William Pitt the younger became Prime Minister. Pitt was only three years older than the Prince of Wales, but the contrast in their characters could not have been greater.

An obvious difference was that Pitt remained a bachelor all his life. The Prince of Wales was no innocent, even when he first met Mrs Fitzherbert. His relationships with women caused his parents particular grief. Mary Robinson, nicknamed 'Perdita', was an actress and a writer as well as being the mistress of the Prince of Wales. She met the prince in 1779 when he was seventeen and she was twenty-one. He gave her a cheque for £20,000, but it was worth nothing until he came of age himself. By that time, he had lost interest in her. She got her own back by selling his letters to the newspapers.

Elizabeth Milbanke, later Viscountess Melbourne, was one of the prince's earliest mistresses. She gave birth to a son called George, the year before the prince married Mrs Fitzherbert. (Elizabeth's legitimate son, the second Viscount Melbourne, later became prime minister under Queen Victoria.) Grace Dalrymple was an even earlier mistress of the prince, as her daughter, Georgina, was born a couple of years before Elizabeth Milbanke's child. Grace was married to Dr Elliott, a sought-after London physician. Having discarded her elderly husband, she became the mistress of several titled men, and it is not certain that Georgina, despite her name, was the Prince of Wales's child.

The philandering was briefly interrupted when Maria Fitzherbert came to London. The prince immediately fell in love again, threatening suicide if Maria would not marry him.

Although the granddaughter of a baronet, Mrs Fitzherbert did not have the right background (she was six years older than the prince, and twice widowed to boot) nor did she move in the right stratum of society ever to be accepted as a suitable wife for a Prince of Wales. Moreover, she was a Roman Catholic. Nevertheless, the prince found a desperate young clergyman, the Revd John Burt, who was prepared to do the job of marrying them, and the deed was done in December 1785. The secret marriage was the talk of the town, but few knew for sure that it had taken place. The couple could not officially live together, but Maria would regularly go through the charade of accepting a lift home in the prince's carriage after an evening out.

The honeymoon was soon over. Maria disliked the prince's political ally, Fox, and in the spring of 1787 Fox denied the rumours of a secret marriage on the floor of the House of Commons. Furious with the prince for allowing this, Maria temporarily cut off relations with him. They were reconciled after Fox's strategy had worked and George had been granted an increased allowance by Parliament.

The first time a regency was proposed, it had nothing to do with George III's mental health, but with a physical illness, and the choice of regent was between his wife, his mother, and his uncle Cumberland. It was not until 1788 that a question mark appeared over the king's state of mind, and it began to be said that his son, the Prince of Wales, might have to be called on to stand in for him. The Prince Regent, as we are used to thinking of him, would spend as many years ruling on his father's behalf as he did as king in his own right.

At one time, the prince had shown some promise as a monarch, having charm, a certain amount of artistic talent, and a little interest in the process of government. By the time his reign became a real possibility, he had begun to display the worst traits of his Hanoverian ancestors. As well as an excessive interest in the opposite sex, he showed a lack of self-discipline when it came to eating, drinking and entertainment. Georgiana, Duchess of Devonshire, described him as 'inclined to be too fat and looks too much like a woman in men's cloaths'. His debts were still mounting.

Maria Fitzherbert was considered by many to be good for the prince. Although their life together in Brighton was extravagant, it was noted that he was drinking less and was altogether in a better humour, winning the approval of his former critics. This of course would not last.

The prince's fortunes changed somewhat when his father began to show signs of serious mental instability. In October 1788, Fanny Burney was one of those who recorded the curious state of the king's health. The ailment, though it affected his mental condition, also had physical symptoms, and doctors believed he was suffering from gout. Eventually he became violent and seemed to be hallucinating. The public got to hear of it, and by 11 November the papers were denying rumours of George III's death. He was moved out of the royal apartments at Windsor Castle, to his palace at Kew, where the maverick Dr Francis Willis was called upon to treat him, very much as a last resort.

In the meantime, the Prince of Wales had begun to be hopeful of taking on the regency. The Duke of York, who had recently returned from a long period overseas, was not a good influence on him. Having successfully subdued his mother the queen, the heir apparent ordered everyone about, and the household descended into anarchy. Fox was pressing for him to be appointed regent, and Pitt reluctantly agreed to introduce a bill for this purpose, knowing it was political suicide. The prince's response to the crisis was to declare a devotion to his father that he had never shown in practice: 'I tremble at the thought of doing anything which may in the smallest degree endanger the agitating of His Majesty's mind.'

The political machinations that occupied the government from November 1788 to February 1789 ended with the king's miraculous recovery, attributed by many to Dr Willis's unconventional methods. The Prince of Wales ended by looking foolish. During the period of his father's illness, he had encouraged the political opposition, demanded favours of Pitt and other party leaders, drawn up lists of those to be made peers and bishops (there were plans to make Mrs Fitzherbert a duchess), and he and his brother had openly made fun of the king during their drinking sessions at Carlton House. By mid-February, there was no doubt that the king was substantially recovered, and the Regency Bill was abandoned. The queen, meanwhile, looked forward to an opportunity for revenge on her eldest son for his unforgivable behaviour during the winter.

In March, the brothers were both cheered *and* jeered in the streets. At the thanksgiving service for the king's recovery, in April, they showed disrespect for the occasion by laughing together and noisily eating biscuits during the sermon in St Paul's.

The prince managed to retain the good opinion of at least part of the population, and when, in 1792, he made an impressive maiden speech in the House of Lords, even the politicians became hopeful of a new leader in the making. When war broke out with the French, he begged to be allowed to undertake military service, likening himself to the Black Prince, though they could hardly have been more different. He pleaded with his father that he was prepared 'to shed the last drop of my blood in support of Your Majesty's person'. In 1793, he was appointed colonel to the Tenth Light Dragoons, but he resented the lowliness of his position: 'my birth, rank, consequence, education, age and time of life is all to go for nothing.'

At this time, the prince remained 'attached' to Mrs Fitzherbert, but on seeing his brother, the Duke of York, improve his fortunes by marrying Princess Frederica of Prussia, a girl of whom everyone approved, George began to rethink his position. His mounting debts were among the many causes of friction between him and Maria. At the same time, he had not given up other women, and the Welsh-descended actress, Anna Maria Crouch, was one of those who caught his eye.

It was the arrival on the scene of Frances, Lady Jersey, that finally brought the fiasco of the Fitzherbert marriage to an end. This thoroughly unpleasant woman made it her business to come between the Prince of Wales and his illegal wife, as she would later come between him and his legal wife. By 1794, he had made up his mind to abandon Maria permanently.

With such a history, it came as a great relief to the king and queen when their eldest son decided to take a wife and settle down. They must have heard the rumours about his relationship with Mrs Fitzherbert. Having tired of Maria, George took advantage of the fact that he was not legally bound to her, and looked around for someone more suitable to bear his royal children. Even before his marriage, he had complained to his brother that for him 'the choice of wife was indeed a lottery and one from the wheel of which I did not, at least at present, intend to draw a ticket'.

His fancy hit upon Caroline of Brunswick, a cousin he had never seen and whose personal habits turned out to be as coarse as his own. Although keen for him to marry, his parents were not entirely happy with his choice, the queen in particular being very distressed by rumours she had heard about the princess's loose morals. No doubt his mother's opposition helped decide the Prince of Wales on what turned out to be a ruinous course.

The story of the couple's first meeting has passed into legend. The princess was 'welcomed' by the spiteful Lady Jersey, who saw to it that she did not look her best. The prince, on seeing her, asked for a glass of brandy. The marriage took place immediately, in April 1795, and it was over almost before it started. The prince spent their wedding night lying drunk in the fireplace. In diaries whose contents have since become public knowledge, he claimed that he only slept with his bride two or three times. That proved enough to enable her to conceive, and the result was their daughter, Charlotte, on whom the prince doted. Caroline, who was as disenchanted with her husband as he was with her, was nevertheless put out at being sidelined by the royal mistress. If she hoped for any improvement in her situation after the birth of Princess Charlotte, she was to be disappointed. Care of the child was taken out of her hands almost immediately. The rest of her new family were as disdainful of her as her husband was, and only her father-in-law, the king, showed any sympathy for her, admonishing his son for not making more effort to repair the marital rift that had so quickly deepened.

George's attitude to his family was contradictory. He attempted to settle down to domestic life with Mrs Fitzherbert, both before his marriage to Caroline, and again afterwards, when a brief reconciliation found him living in Brighton with Maria. In his will, written shortly after his daughter's birth, when he imagined himself to be mortally ill, he referred to Maria as 'the wife of my heart and soul'. Foolish as Caroline was, she recognized that the real threat to her status was not Lady Jersey but Mrs Fitzherbert. For her part, Maria refused to refer to Caroline as Princess of Wales, a title she presumably regarded as hers by right. In 1799, it was falsely rumoured that Mrs Fitzherbert had died. George was inconsolable, writing to her to check that it was not true. 'I am wrapped up in you entirely,' he claimed. 'After 17 years' attachment nothing can alter me, shake me or change me.'

After their final parting in 1807, he treated Maria as badly as he had previously done, yet he is said to have kept every one of her letters. Clearly he was capable of deep feeling. The fact that his one legitimate child was not a son does not seem to have made him any less fond of her, nor did he consider her unfit to succeed him as monarch. His love for little Princess Charlotte of Wales was equalled only by his hatred for Charlotte's mother, his legal wife, and he ensured that Caroline was given as little access as possible to the child. Having introduced a strict regime for Charlotte's care, he changed her governess when he thought the incumbent was getting too friendly with the Princess of Wales.

Unfeeling as this seems, the Prince of Wales was deeply affected by the death of his youngest sister, Princess Amelia, in 1810. Amelia had been his goddaughter as well as his sister, and had found in him a sympathetic confidant when she launched herself into a hopeless love affair with Charles Fitzroy, a courtier who was descended from one of Charles II's many liaisons. In general, the prince got on well with his sisters, especially Princess Mary, who in 1816, at the age of thirty-eight, stepped out of line and married her cousin Prince William Frederick, becoming Duchess of Gloucester.

As Prince of Wales, George was one of very few who took an active interest in the principality as well as in the income he derived from it. It may be surmised that he saw an opportunity to recapture some of the popularity he had lost in the country as a whole. In 1806, he visited Shrewsbury, and went from there into Wales, where he planted a tree near Llandrinio in Montgomeryshire. He was accompanied by Sir Richard Puleston, who earned the right to display the Prince of Wales's feathers as a result. (The attraction for the prince may well have been Sir Richard's wife, Emma.)

The Welsh had the potential to become George's own private following, just as they had been for the Black Prince and for Richard II and as they would later be for Edward VIII. George needed such a coterie because he had already aroused the disapproval of Pitt's government, and the nation, by his debauched and spendthrift conduct. Pitt proposed that Parliament limit the powers of the prince in the event of his becoming regent, particularly in financial terms. The king's mental health had improved in time to prevent the Regency Bill becoming law. It was not until February 1811 that the prince was called upon to take on the full powers of a regent. His father had suffered a recurrence of his mental illness in October 1810, and this time he did not recover.

The Prince Regent spent much of his regency looking for opportunities to get rid of his wife, accusing her of adultery (of which she was guilty) and even of having an illegitimate child of her own (of which she was almost certainly innocent). By the time George III died, in 1820, the prince had lost his only daughter. His beloved Charlotte had died in childbirth three years earlier, less than two years after marrying Prince Leopold of Saxe-Coburg-Saalfeld. Having apparently resigned himself to his childless state, George IV made no attempt to divorce Caroline and remarry, though now might have been a good time to persuade Parliament of his case. Instead, he settled down to the business of ruling for the few years he had left.

The new king was dismissed by the Duke of Wellington as 'a blockhead'. One of the most momentous events of his early reign was the news of the death of Napoleon in exile on St Helena. When told that his greatest enemy was dead, George immediately assumed that the reference was to his wife, and was disappointed to find that it was not so. When Caroline did, in fact, die, a couple of months later, he remarked that 'the blessing which the protecting hand of God in his mercy has bestowed upon me in this recent event is so great I even yet can hardly bring myself to believe that it is really so'. In the same year, his former mistress, Lady Jersey, passed away.

The coronation, from which Caroline had been turned away, was celebrated throughout the land. At the Parys Mountain copper mine near Amlwch, the 'Coronation' shaft was opened, and, despite several injuries as a result of gunpowder blasting, 1,000 miners drank the new king's health, with the local bigwigs feasting in a marquee nearby. At Holyhead later in the year, on his way to Ireland, the king transferred from the royal yacht to the steam-packet 'Lightning' in order to complete his voyage against the wind. It was here that the news of the queen's death reached him, and he was advised to make some pretence of mourning by taking a short break at Plas Newydd, home of the Marquess of Anglesey, the man who had lost his leg at Waterloo six years earlier.

In 1822, with the encouragement of his friend Sir Walter Scott, George IV became the first reigning monarch to visit Scotland since Charles II. He lapped up the pageantry that welcomed him, taking pleasure in the opportunity to dress up in a kilt and portraying himself as a true descendant of the Stuart dynasty. He spent over £1,000 on his 'Royal Stewart' tartan costume with an outfitter based in Princes Street, Edinburgh, a thoroughfare that had originally been named after George and his brother. In all, he spent three weeks in his second kingdom, a fine precedent for future British monarchs. He also visited Ireland and Hanover, both places having been deprived of royal visits for many years.

His health was already deteriorating, the number of his years curtailed by the consequences of riotous living. Massively over-weight, addicted to laudanum, and showing signs of dementia, he died in 1830, to be succeeded by his brother, William, Duke of Clarence (the oldest person ever to accede to the British throne, at the age of 65). The George IV Hotel in Criccieth, built in the same year, is a testimony to the pride taken by at least some of the Welsh population in their former prince, but it was not generally shared. The day after the king's funeral, *The Times*, no less, printed this startlingly outspoken statement: 'There never was an individual less regretted by his fellow creatures than this deceased King . . . of all known beings the most selfish. Nothing remains to be said about George IV but to pay, as pay we must, for his profusion.'

A few weeks before his death, the king had admitted to his chaplain that there was much he regretted in his early life, but protested that 'as king I have always tried to benefit my subjects. I have shown mercy to others, and hope that it will be shown to me.' There is no doubt that he was a soft-hearted man, even if his strongest sentiments were reserved for himself.

William IV, like his elder brother, had no legitimate children, and the throne passed in 1837 to the nearest heir, Princess Victoria, daughter of the Earl of Kent.

Bertie

The longest-serving Prince of Wales of all time was Prince Albert Edward, the eldest son of Queen Victoria. When he took the title, a month after his birth (9 November 1841), there had not been a Prince of Wales for over twenty years, and the public – those who remembered George IV in his heyday – must have waited with bated breath to see how the new young prince would compare. As it happened, there was more than a touch of his great-uncle in Bertie's make-up.

Almost as soon as the prince was born, *The Cambrian*, an English-language newspaper published in Wales, printed a letter decrying a proposal to teach Welsh to the boy who would soon be Prince of Wales. It was suggested that the language, with its unfamiliar sounds, was beyond the grasp of any civilized person. It would be unnatural, the letter continued, to force the prince into such a study. The fact that such an argument was taking place in the 1840s makes it difficult to understand the attempts, later in the same century, to obliterate the Welsh language in schools. Of one thing we can be reasonably sure, however: the Prince of Wales played no part in the debate.

Instead of being taught Welsh, Bertie was educated at home by tutors such as Henry Birch, a former master at Eton, and Frederick Gibbs, a Cambridge lecturer. His course of study was personally supervised by his father, the Prince Consort, and was designed to test him. Overseeing it all was Albert's own former tutor, Baron von Stockmar. The Prince of Wales was not, however, an academic by nature. Although he embarked on three university courses, the first at Edinburgh, the second at Christ Church (the most exclusive of the Oxford colleges), and

Edward Albert, Prince of Wales, son of Queen Victoria. From a Victorian print.

finally a stint at Trinity College, Cambridge (where the present Prince of Wales would later study), he never took a degree.

In 1860, he was allowed by his parents to represent them in a visit to Canada. It says something about the young man's impetuous nature that he attempted to accept an invitation from the famous tightrope-walker, Blondin, to accompany him across Niagara Falls! Albert and Victoria were unimpressed. On his return to Britain, they gave him little personal credit for the good impression he had made. They did not want to encourage the populist aspect of his character.

By the time he came of age, Bertie's father was dead, and many blamed Prince Albert's last illness on a chill he had caught while visiting Madingley Hall near Cambridge to administer discipline to his wayward son. Bertie had been caught in the act of fornication with a young actress, Nellie Clifden, while on a short course with the army in Ireland, and the story had taken some time to reach his parents. The incident helped set the tone for the remainder of his career as Prince of Wales.

As shown by early photographs and portraits, Bertie was not a handsome youth. His chubby cheeks are much in evidence. By growing whiskers to disguise his downy complexion, he only succeeded in making himself look prematurely middle-aged. His dumpy figure seems to have been inherited from his mother, who quickly put on weight after the birth of her first few children. Good looks were not the basis of his ability to attract the opposite sex.

Less than eighteen months after his father's death, he was married off to a Danish princess, Alexandra. At the time of their wedding, in St George's Chapel, Windsor, 'Alix' was nineteen to Bertie's twenty-one. It has been traditional for royal children to be married young, and in the Victorian era teenage brides were far from unusual. Although Bertie met his future wife on several occasions and expressed satisfaction with her as a potential bride, he followed royal etiquette and proposed to her according to strict instructions received from above. Misspent youth cut short is not necessarily a good preparation for a lifetime of public duty, and any hopes that Bertie would 'settle down' after his marriage were soon dashed, particularly in the absence of a father figure to watch over him.

Alix would prove a loyal wife and a good mother to the couple's five children. However, at least in the beginning, she shared some of Bertie's light-heartedness, which, in the end, made her a less than ideal partner for an undisciplined young man. There was no shortage of opportunities for social activity, in view of the fact that Queen Victoria remained isolated in her mourning and preferred not to fulfil public engagements. The prince travelled on her behalf, notably to Ireland and Egypt, where he made a good impression through sheer bonhomie. Alix did not always accompany him. Bertie, never trusted by his mother with responsibility, would later, as king, reject any idea of involving his wife in the process of government.

In London, the Prince and Princess of Wales had Marlborough House as their official residence. In the country, they were to live at Sandringham, a run-down property purchased by Prince Albert as a shooting-lodge and in need of a face-lift. 'Sandringham Time', an hour ahead of the rest of the country, was established by the prince to allow more time for sporting activities. The young couple were outwardly happy, and enjoyed both sport and society. Bertie, having been excluded from some of London's gambling clubs, opened one of his own, the Marlborough Club, to get around the problem. His wife did not openly complain. On the contrary, for as long as she could, she joined in his social activities, and they entertained on a sumptuous scale. Children began to arrive within a year of their marriage, and the male succession was secured with the birth of a son, Prince Albert Victor. Another son, Prince George, was born on 3 June 1865. It was in this boy's hands that the future of the monarchy truly lay.

When Bertie reverted to his pre-marital pleasure-loving state and lost interest in his wife and children, the honeymoon was well and truly over. He continued to take mistresses, and Alix was obliged to tolerate them. For her to have confided in a journalist, as one of her successors later did, would have been out of the question. She was obliged to suffer in silence as women like Alice Keppel and Lillie Langtry accompanied her husband to private social engagements. In 1870, a scandal blew up when Bertie was called on to give evidence in the Mordaunt divorce case. Lady Mordaunt, a regular visitor to Marlborough House, claimed to have slept with the Prince of

Wales, among others, and her husband, Sir Charles, attempted to divorce her for adultery on the strength of this boasting. Fortunately for the prince, the evidence of his intimacy with Lady Mordaunt was non-existent. It seems he was actually innocent in this case; but it did nothing to improve his reputation, nor his relationships with his mother and his wife.

Bertie was not a monster. His vices were relatively harmless, and he was never guilty of the excesses practised by some of his predecessors, either as Prince of Wales or as king. He was capable of great love and devotion. It rather seems that his faults were those of his mother's ancestors. This is ironic when we consider that Victoria's disappointment in him was largely caused by his failure to resemble his father. Albert had been an upright man with a strict moral code that he attempted to instil in his much-loved children, but no one can have forgotten that he introduced the style of Christmas celebrations we enjoy today, the colourful cards and the decorated trees. It gives the lie to any idea that he was a humourless martinet. Victoria had gradually, after some degree of marital strife, come to see Albert's administrative abilities, and to rely on them. When her son failed to toe the line, however, she did not recognize his independent streak as having any potential value. Her attempts to build his character – the kind of character *she* wanted – were guaranteed to fail, unaccompanied as they were by any real delegation of responsibility.

This does not mean that the prince did not carry out official duties. It was just after Bertie had opened the International Exhibition of 1871 that an attack of typhoid almost killed him, prompting someone (though probably not the future Poet Laureate, Alfred Austin, who is usually accused of it) to pen the much-mocked lines, 'Across the wires the electric message came, / He is no better, he is much the same'. Throughout his illness, it was his faithful wife who kept a bedside vigil. Following his recovery, the prince appeared to turn over a new leaf, taking an increased interest in his domestic arrangements and turning away, for a while, from the lifestyle that had begun to make him an object of scorn in the media and among politicians. His five children began to claim more of his attention. A sixth child had been born and died the same day during this period of domestic crisis.

Victorian manufacturing companies did not hesitate to use the royal seal of approval. This advertisement features the future King Edward VII.

Such cycles of behaviour continued. The prince's visit to India in 1875–6 was long remembered. He spent four months travelling the country, named a bridge after his wife, met regional potentates, and paved the way for his mother's inauguration as Empress of India in 1876. He travelled up the Ganges in a galley decorated with sea-horses to be received by the maharajah of Benares, and both men were carried in silver chairs up the hill to the maharajah's castle. Gladstone and his government were impressed with the report they received on his return.

During the prince's absence, however, the Princess of Wales had received an unwelcome visit from Lord Randolph Churchill and Lady Aylesford, threatening to name Bertie in yet another divorce case. The queen learned of the scandal, as did the public, and the triumph of the Indian visit was forgotten. Bertie and Alix ensured that Lord Randolph and Lady Churchill were ostracized by polite society, but their own marriage was in the doldrums.

It was in 1877 that Bertie first met Lillie Langtry, the actress popularly known as 'the Jersey lily'. Langtry allegedly fell out with the prince after she became too lively at a party and tipped ice down his back. Alice Keppel, on the other hand, was a mistress who came to be regarded with affection by the Princess of Wales. In their later years, Mrs Keppel followed the couple everywhere. Like another Princess of Wales, Caroline of Ansbach, Alix had decided favourites among her husband's female companions – those she regarded as being a good, rather than a bad, influence on him.

Throughout the 1880s and 1890s the Prince of Wales carried out a series of exhausting public engagements. In the meantime, his children were growing up. His eldest daughter, Princess Louise, was married in 1889. By 1890, when he was forced to appear as a witness in court at the libel case involving Sir William Gordon–Cumming, the Prince of Wales had renewed his reputation as a playboy. When, towards the end of 1891, she learned of the scandal surrounding Bertie's relationship with Lady Brooke (later Daisy, Countess of Warwick), Alexandra was ready to call a halt to the marriage, if she had been able. The 'babbling' Lady Brooke, granddaughter of a viscount, had effectively used her relationship with the Prince of Wales as a cover for an affair with Lord Charles Beresford. The song 'Daisy, Daisy', was inspired by the countess's activities; as well as the notoriety she received for her extramarital relationships, she was a notable philanthropist. It has been said that her social-istic leanings were what eventually turned the prince against her.

In 1892, a family tragedy brought the royal couple closer together again. Bertie's eldest son, Prince Albert Victor, Duke of Clarence, died suddenly aged twenty-eight. The prince, though dearly loved, had been a trial to his parents, copying the worst of his father's behaviour, associating with unsavoury companions and attempting to take a Roman Catholic bride. His parents identified someone more suitable in the shape of a distant cousin, Princess May of Teck; May's mother, Princess Mary Adelaide, was related through her father to Bertie and through her mother to Alix. No sooner had the prince been found a suitable fiancée to take him in hand, however, than he contracted influenza and died of pneumonia, just as his younger brother, George, was recovering from a bout of typhoid.

As Prince of Wales, Bertie paid few visits, official or other-wise, to his principality. The first was as a small child, aboard the royal yacht when it moored at Caernarfon. He was not intro-duced to his Welsh subjects. Some years after their marriage, Bertie and Alix travelled to Ireland via Wales, where they were enthusiastically received. Yet a few years later, Queen Victoria was taking her son to task for not visiting his adopted country more often. In 1894, he attended the National Eisteddfod at Caernarfon, and was initiated into the Gorsedd of bards. On this occasion, Alix accompanied him, and the Nantlle brass band played appropriate music as the couple sailed by on the royal yacht.

In January 1901, the apparently immortal Victoria finally passed away, and it was time for the Prince of Wales to take the Crown, for which his mother had never fully prepared him. After so many years waiting in the wings, it must have been something of a shock to a man of his age, a shock compounded by the death of his elder sister, Vicky, a few months later. Vicky, of course, was the Kaiser's mother, and her death left Wilhelm II of Germany freer than ever to indulge his delusions of grandeur.

A fortnight before the coronation was due to take place in June 1902, King Edward VII was taken seriously ill again, this time with appendicitis, and needed a major operation to save his life. The state of his health improved enough for him to be crowned later in the year. On New Year's Day, 1903, he was declared Emperor of India in a 'durbar' at Delhi, and he continued to travel the world, often (but not always) with his loyal queen by his side.

In 1905, as king, he granted Cardiff the status of a city, a status whose centenary has just been celebrated without much mention of the role played by Edward VII. The city does, however, honour his memory in the name of one of its major thoroughfares, King Edward VII Avenue. It was not until 1907 that the king paid a visit to Cardiff in person, and this would be the first visit made to the city by a reigning monarch since Charles I came in the seventeenth century to muster his flagging support. The city did not become Wales's official capital until 1955, when it was known that the Empire Games were to be held there.

Edward VII was a king who looked outside the British Isles, to Europe and the British Empire. His cosmopolitan attitudes made him a good ambassador for the country, though his willingness to ignore the advice of professional diplomats also brought him some criticism. The *entente cordiale* he had built up with the French did not endear him to some other European governments. In 1909, however, the visit of the king and queen to Bertie's nephew, Kaiser Wilhelm II, in Germany helped stave off war for a few more years.

A political crisis later in the year ended with the king being forced to threaten to create additional peers in order to get the Budget through the House of Lords and thus keep the Liberal government in office. It was the most active a monarch had been in politics for many years. His concern over the affair contributed to the general failure of his health, and in the early months of 1910, he had a serious attack of bronchitis while holidaying at Biarritz in the company of Alice Keppel. His health did not improve when he returned to London, and for the first time he was unable to welcome Queen Alexandra in person when she set foot on British soil after her own Mediterranean holiday. Two days later, the king suffered a series of heart attacks, and it was clear that his life was almost at an end. Mrs Keppel was sent for by the queen. Prince George, himself now Prince of Wales, arrived to say that the king's horse had won at Kempton Park. Edward VII died later that evening.

He is remembered as a good-natured, if not a good, king. The sins that seemed so heinous when practised by other Princes of Wales have been lessened in history's eyes by Bertie's reputation for general good humour and ability to get on with people. These are qualities we particularly value in our royal family.

King George V and his Heir

It was sheer accident that the future George V ever held the title of Prince of Wales. It should, by rights, have gone to his elder brother, Prince Albert Victor. The accident cannot be said to have been an unfortunate one, because Albert Victor, or Eddy as he was familiarly known, was a very suspect character. If only half the stories about him are true, he was far worse than his father in terms of excessive behaviour.

Despite this, the two brothers were inseparable, and George was heartbroken when, in 1892, Eddy suddenly contracted influenza and died, just after celebrating his twenty-eighth birthday. Himself recovering from a serious illness at the time, George was kneeling by his brother's bedside. He was devastated at the loss of his lifelong friend and companion.

In their early youth, the boys had been educated together, their tutor being John Neale Dalton, a canon of St George's Chapel, Windsor, and chaplain to their grandmother, Queen Victoria, at Sandringham. Canon Dalton protested that he could do little with the raw material he was given, particularly with Eddy. From the age of twelve, George's career in the navy was marked out, and he received little formal education from that point on. Both boys were sent to Dartmouth College, largely because they could not bear to be apart, and Dalton went with them. It was said that the only privilege they enjoyed was to be given a room to themselves. This in itself was an enormous privilege, which must have marked them out from their fellow naval cadets. Now they had a new teacher, the ominously named Mr Lawless.

George took to the sea well, becoming even better travelled than his adventurous father. Dalton remained with the boys

The future George V, as Duke of York, at his wedding to May of Teck in 1893. They would become Prince and Princess of Wales in 1901.

when they boarded HMS *Bacchante* in 1882, the last time they would be together. The purpose of Dalton's presence was mainly to ensure that they were not led astray. Under Lawless, George excelled at mathematics. Speaking of his naval training in later years, he said that the three qualities it had instilled in him were truthfulness, obedience and zeal. During the 1880s, he served in North America and the West Indies, becoming a junior officer on his nineteenth birthday. It was while serving in Malta that he became acquainted with Princess Marie of Edinburgh, his first cousin. Only the disapproval of Marie's mother, a Russian grand duchess, prevented them from marrying. While in Malta, he also grew the beard that would be part of his distinctive image for the rest of his life.

When Eddy died, George not only inherited his position as second in line to the throne; he also, in what was becoming the traditional manner, inherited his fiancée. May of Teck had little in common with Eddy, but she and George made a good couple. Many people today have a clear memory of them as king and queen, and the overall impression of Queen Mary (as she was later known) is of a stately, dignified woman who seemed to dominate the royal family. Yet her own son would later say that 'she was a different person away from *him*', seeming to suggest that it was actually George who not only held the reins of the marriage, but dictated the behaviour of those around him.

Following Eddy's death, Queen Victoria had given George the title of Duke of York. He did not leave the navy immediately on his marriage, but continued on active service until 1898. The prince's duties as captain of HMS *Melampus* included presiding at religious services, something that must have appealed to both the authoritarian and the moralist in him. He had inherited his strong religious faith from his mother.

What kind of man was this, the first monarch to have lived out his life in the age of photography and sound recording, so that much of it is still available to public view? W. T. Stead, writing at the beginning of George's reign as king, was candid: 'For a young man who speaks so much, and who speaks so well, there is a surprising absence of nonsense in his writings and his speeches.' At the same time, Stead was concerned that the new king had a tendency to jingoism and was politically naive, perhaps not ready to tackle the imminent crisis over Irish Home Rule.

Over the years, he had the opportunity to visit much of the British Empire, and this was always at the forefront of his thoughts. A cousin of both the Tsar of Russia and the Kaiser of Germany, he bore a close physical resemblance to both. When he looked at them, it must have been difficult to remember that, in matters of politics and specifically war, he was answerable to Parliament for his actions. It is well attested that he did not care for the most influential of his prime ministers, David Lloyd George, the 'Welsh wizard'. The king considered him both obstinate and deceitful, and no doubt Lloyd George had an equally low opinion of the king. In 1911, the wizard would write to his wife from Balmoral saying that both George V and his queen were 'hostile to the bone' to anyone who tried to improve the lot of the working classes.

George V's time as Prince of Wales was relatively short, ten years sandwiched in between his nine years as Duke of York and his twenty-six year reign as king. By the time the title came to him, it must have taken some getting used to. When his father took the throne, George was a mature man of thirty-five and the father of four children. He had had plenty of time, in his early life, to grasp the idea that his father, not he, was Prince of Wales. A ten-month gap was deliberately left between Bertie's elevation to the throne as King Edward VII and George's investiture as Prince of Wales, so as make the change more gradual. George took the title on 9 November 1901, his father's sixtieth birthday, but there was no investiture ceremony involved. That practice seemed to have come to an end in the seventeenth century. It was Lloyd George who would have the idea of reviving it – not for George, Prince of Wales, but for his eldest son.

That George took his duties as Prince of Wales seriously is not to be doubted; he took everything seriously, particularly duty. In his youth, he had sown some wild oats. There had been rumours of romance while he was in the navy, but any such escapades were kept quiet by the media, and the evidence suggests that they were quite tame by today's standards. As a naval cadet, he certainly flirted with women, and he was definitely still in love with Marie of Edinburgh when May of

Teck was bequeathed to him by his brother, but he had never become the roué that Eddy was rumoured to have been.

George had loved Eddy so much that he may well have regarded it as not only a duty, but an honour, to take on this new fiancée. He fulfilled his part of the bargain well, being a faithful husband and a father who did his best to guide his off-spring in the 'right' path – which was not necessarily the easiest for them. The eldest boy, always known by his last forename of David, was only seven years old when George became Prince of Wales in 1901. He may not have understood that he would one day hold the same title, though no doubt it would have been pointed out to him more than once.

George V did not fail to take an interest in Wales. It was on the occasion of his marriage to May of Teck, in 1893, that Welsh gold was used for the first time in a royal wedding ring. Political upheaval would later make it expedient for him to visit the south Wales coalfield, where severe disruption was being caused by poor industrial relations. He did not, however, embrace the Welsh as his subjects in any special way, and did little to make up for the neglect shown the principality by Edward VII, who had visited so rarely during his sixty-year career as Prince of Wales. 'England is good enough for me,' George is once supposed to have said, responding to the criticism that he was unwilling to travel as extensively as his father had done. There is no real suggestion that he had a clearer picture of Wales as an entity than his father did. The importance, for him, of the title was that it identified him unequivocally as the heir apparent (something a Prince of Wales must always be).

For a Prince of Wales to become king normally involves losing his father. George, writing in his diary just after his father's death in 1910, said: 'I have lost my best friend and the best of fathers.' Very different the two men may have been, but they had a good relationship. King Edward VII had done his best to ensure that his son was not excluded from the business of government as he had been by his mother. George was seen by everyone as the solid, dependable sort, as indeed was his wife.

By the time George became king, Canon Dalton had moved on, and was married to a Welshwoman. In 1902, the canon presented a paper to the Colonial Institute, in which he sug-gested that many of the population of the British Empire were being deprived of a say in its government. 'The most natural and simple solution', he said, 'would be for the Imperial Parliament to delegate to *the English, Scotch, and Irish* people the management of their own national and domestic affairs, while retaining the supreme control of Imperial affairs in its own hands, and to it then the Colonial representatives could be admitted' (my italics). Wales, presumably, would continue to be treated as part of England. What the canon wrote reflected what the more conservative section of the Welsh population was happy to accept.

George V's travels with the navy and his official visits to distant corners of the British Empire had not been wasted. When, in 1911, he became the first (and only) British monarch to attend a coronation durbar in India, confirming him as emperor, he announced that the seat of the imperial govern-ment would be transferred from London to Delhi. It was a decision that was not welcomed by Conservative politicians at home, but the result was probably to make the empire last a little longer than it should have done. On a previous visit to the subcontinent, as Prince of Wales, George had noted how badly the natives were treated, and had looked forward to a day when he could do something to help them.

The new king had borne the title of Prince of Wales with dignity. On his accession it was automatically assumed that the title would pass to his eldest son, David, and public expectation was not disappointed. The idea of a public investiture ceremony, however, was a radical one. Lloyd George, perhaps conscious of how his own commitment to Wales had appeared to dwindle as well as of the growing popular movement for independence (Plaid Cymru was founded in 1925), put the idea to the new king and queen almost as soon as they began their reign. He must already have had it in his mind, in order to have been able to organize such a major undertaking as early as 1911. The concept of holding the ceremony, and holding it in Wales, though it seems quite natural now, would have been very strange to the royal family at the time.

The new prince had been born on 23 June 1894, at White Lodge, Richmond, and had immediately become a favourite of his great-grandmother, Queen Victoria, who took him for carriage-rides and fed him sweet tea from a spoon. Queen

Alexandra, known for her love of children, also had a soft spot for her eldest grandson, and encouraged him by keeping some of his naughtier moments a secret from his parents.

H. P. Hansell, who had tutored one of Victoria's younger sons, the Duke of Connaught, was appointed to take charge of the prince's early education, and they developed a close relationship despite the boy's often wayward behaviour. While visiting Bangor as a child, he escaped with his sister Mary from the royal party, and climbed to the top of a nearby tower for a bird's-eye view of the crowd. At that time, although it could be predicted that he would one day be Prince of Wales, the title remained his father's.

'King George has already earned the gratitude of his millions of subjects,' gushed W. and L. Townsend in their 1929 'biography' of the Prince of Wales. 'His simple characteristics and warm earnestness are well known. H.R.H. is a different type of man altogether. He is a King of the future.' Throughout this eulogy, 'England' is used as a synonym for the United Kingdom.

With unusual candour, the Townsends mention that 'the people of Wales were not wholly satisfied' with arrangements for David's investiture, implying that this was the only thing the Welsh did not like about having an English prince. 'The Welsh people were agitating', they admit, 'for the Investiture to take place within the Principality.' Several venues were considered, including Chester. Naturally, the people of that city were disappointed that the royal family failed to favour them with a special visit in which the earldom could have been conferred. The weight of public engagements was claimed as a reason for this omission.

The selection of Caernarfon Castle, close to Lloyd George's own home town as well as the traditional site of the original making of an English Prince of Wales, was far from a foregone conclusion. In the end, it won out, and that choice caused no small inconvenience to the royals. Caernarfon is and was a very small town, and road access at the time was poor (though of course the national rail network had not then been reduced to its present parlous state).

The ceremony took place on 13 July 1911, and a good photographic record of the occasion survives. The prince was decked

The ceremony on 13 July 1911. The prince was decked out in what he himself called a 'preposterous rig' of purple velvet surcoat trimmed with fur and purple silk sash.

out in white satin knee breeches, white silk stockings and what he himself called a 'preposterous rig' of purple velvet surcoat trimmed with fur, and purple silk sash. He had inherited his father's dislike of the ceremonial. A special set of regalia was designed, using Welsh gold. (A new, less 'olde worlde' set would be created for Prince Charles in 1969.) The Investiture Medal was designed by the sculptor Goscombe John, who had worked under William Burges on the decoration of Castell Coch.

We can get the flavour of the occasion by looking at photographs of another investiture endured by the prince a month earlier, that of the Order of the Garter. The Garter had been presented to every adult Prince of Wales since the Black Prince, and since 1805 it has been automatically bestowed on the holder of the title at the time of his creation. This ceremony, complete with a similarly theatrical costume, clearly showed the way forward for those charged with the organization of the investiture.

At the Caernarfon ceremony, which lasted an hour and forty minutes in all, the letters patent were read out by Winston Churchill, then Home Secretary, while the new Prince of Wales knelt before his father the king, the latter wearing the uniform of an Admiral of the Fleet. The prince responded to the loyal address, using a few Welsh phrases taught him by Lloyd George, parrot-fashion. Up to now it had not been thought necessary for him to consider learning the language. In his speech, the prince referred to his Christian name, 'David', and his Tudor descent, as evidence of his strong ties to the principality.

As something of an afterthought, the king arranged that the arms of Wales should be added to those of the prince. One might wonder why no one had thought of this before. The following year, on 1 March, his namesake's day, David entertained a group of Welsh bishops at Buckingham Palace, and reassured them of his continued determination to make himself worthy of his title. The bishops were impressed. Here at last, it seemed, was a Prince of Wales deserving of the name.

Having been in Wales so soon after their coronation, the king and queen were obliged to return the following year, this time to visit the scarred valleys of the south, where industrial unrest was rampant. Keir Hardie, the militant Labour MP, had written an open letter to the press in which he pleaded with them not to call on the proprietor of Dowlais ironworks, lest the gesture be misinterpreted as taking the side of the owners. Nowadays they would have been told that such a visit was 'off message'.

They called at the ironworks as part of a three-day tour, during which they laid the foundation stone of the National Museum of Wales at Cardiff. The royal train took them to Lewis Merthyr colliery, the Mines Rescue station at Dinas, and then on a scenic tour of the valleys until they arrived at Dowlais House, former home of Lady Charlotte Guest, the most highly regarded Englishwoman ever to live in Wales. The Dowlais works had been one of the first to go over to making steel. Having passed under a ceremonial arch constructed of coal on entering, the royal couple passed through a steel arch on their way out.

There is no doubt that their eldest son took an interest in the political events going on in his principality. As merely the heir to the throne, it would have been out of the question for David to interfere. Things had changed so much since the end of the Hanoverian line. In 1912, the prince was beginning his career as an undergraduate at Magdalen College, Oxford. His grandfather, King Edward VII, had previously attended Christ Church. David chose Magdalen in the belief that it was less elitist. A special course was devised for him, including history, geography, French, German, English and politics. He was even allowed to select his own friends!

As Prince of Wales, he was one of the most active. He distinguished himself in the eyes of many by not only going to war in 1914, but by insisting on personal visits to the front line, causing great consternation to those given the task of keeping him out of danger. These escapades are obliquely alluded to by the Townsends in the statement that, 'Within certain limits – he was only a young man and impulsive at that – he kept away from the danger-zones in accordance with High Command's express and earnest wishes.' The prince is supposed to have told Lord Kitchener that he did not fear death as he had four younger brothers who could take his place. The nearest he came to dying on active service was when a shell hit his car and killed the driver who was waiting for the prince to finish inspecting the troops.

This gained him some kudos, but the reality was not so heroic. In 1918 he wrote to his lover, Freda Dudley Ward, from

Italy: 'I have to get up at 6.00am tomorrow to go round some trenches up in the mountains, which is a perfectly loathsome thought; I hate having to shove off before 9.00 as I hate getting up before 8.00am at the earliest!!' He concluded the letter with 'tons & tons of my very best love to my darling from her very very very very devoted E.' One wonders what a censor might have made of that, if the prince's letters had been subject to the same restrictions as those of the ordinary soldier.

In the last few months of the war, the Prince of Wales took his seat in the House of Lords with great ceremony. Afterwards began a tour, concentrating on industrial regions of Britain, beginning with south Wales and going on to the mining districts of Cornwall. Like his predecessors, Edward VII and George V, he did a great deal of overseas travelling, particularly in the countries that then formed part of the British Empire. In 1920, just after the war, he embarked on a tour of New Zealand and Australia, accompanied by his younger cousin, Lord Louis Mountbatten (later Earl Mountbatten of Burma). Apparently as a result of an official request, Lord Louis kept a diary in which to record off-stage events. The following year he again accompanied the prince overseas, this time to Japan and India. He kept another diary, this time a more personal one. The diaries were later published and offer 'a most revealing portrait of the Prince of Wales, with all his charm and desire to please, yet with the weaknesses also apparent' (Philip Ziegler). Mountbatten was of course the man many now blame for failing to encourage higher moral standards in his nephew, the present Prince of Wales.

In an intriguing diversion from their catalogue of unmitigated praise for the prince, the Townsends, in a later chapter of their book, dare to ask the question, 'Will the Prince ascend the throne?' What prompted this question was a widespread public perception that David was 'not enthusiastically keen' on his future role. That this was being said so many years before his abdication suggests the presence of fire behind this particular smoke. His grandfather, Edward VII, is supposed to have predicted that David would be Britain's last-ever monarch. 'Those who have some misgivings as to the kind of King he will make', say the Townsends in very bad English, 'fall into a common error of supposing that the Prince would conduct himself the same as he does to-day when later sitting upon the Throne.' They point out that, as Prince of Wales, he enjoyed a freedom that he could not expect to have as king. Naturally, they express confidence that his reign will be a long and glorious one. They also remark that he 'has decided ideas upon the future position Royalty will hold'.

David made himself the champion of the underdog, touring working-class areas such as Scotland and the north of England as well as Wales, asking awkward questions about the welfare of his people. It was the kind of thing the Welsh might have hoped for from their ideal prince, and it was in sharp contrast to the actions of the previous two incumbents. George V had never been a rebel, and Edward VII had departed from the royal norm only in his determination to enjoy himself. Times had changed, and David's reputation as a playboy was tempered by his good showing in other respects. The public was not given the details of his affairs with married women. It was much easier, in those days of limited media communications and greater public respect for the royal family, to restrict the spread of such information.

'A Royal marriage never fails to awaken enthusiasm in the hearts of every English man and woman,' wrote the Townsends, ignoring all evidence to the contrary. When his younger brother, the Duke of York, married Elizabeth Bowes-Lyon in 1923, David stood as best man. As a wedding present, he gave the couple a car, adding a fur stole as a little extra for the bride. This man could have charmed birds from the trees; the personal nature of the present is perhaps an indication that his charm worked less well on the homely Elizabeth than it did on more worldly women.

David was, as one might expect for any Prince of Wales, very eligible. There were not as many European princesses to choose from as there had once been, but he could surely have found a suitable bride close to home, as his father and brother had done. During the war it was rumoured that he was to be engaged to Princess Yolanda of Savoy. This made him popular in Italy. 'Unfortunately a Prince Royal cannot defend himself against rumour,' say the Townsends.

David was more adventurous. He seems to have been attracted by the exotic. While visiting Panama, he was taken to task by some of his companions for selecting a shop-girl as a dance partner at an official function. He had chosen her for her looks and dancing ability rather than her station in life, and this would continue to be his preference. A Lowestoft lifeboatman whom he was presenting with a medal, perhaps sensing the prince's true inclinations, invited him to come to Lowestoft and take his pick of the attractive women to be found there. The crowned heads of Europe never really got a look in.

Whether his preference for married women was something to do with unattainability, or merely, as had been the case with his grandfather, reflected the apparent safety of liaisons with women who had husbands to put up a front and claim any illegitimate children as their own, is uncertain. What is certain is that, by the mid-1930s, he had had relationships with at least two married women: the socialite Freda Dudley Ward (who remained close to him for at least fifteen years) and an American hostess named Thelma, Lady Furness. Born Thelma Morgan, she was one of twins, her sister, Gloria, being the mother of designer Gloria Vanderbilt. Their brother, Harry, was a film actor. Viscount Furness was Thelma's second husband, and it was at their home that David first met another American couple: Ernest Simpson and his wife, Wallis.

This was the woman who was by his side to upset royal protocol as King Edward VIII watched the proclamation of his own accession to the throne from a window of St James's Palace. The still-married Mrs Wallis Simpson had been his companion for the past two years (though Edward denied, right up to his death, that they had been lovers before their marriage).

Like few of his predecessors, David was to become more closely associated with the title of Prince of Wales than he ever was with that of king, holding the former title for twenty-five of his formative years, and the latter for less than twelve months. By the time he took the throne on his father's death in January 1936, he had got into the habit of making an annual St David's Day address to his subjects in Wales. He took the opportunity of his first message as king to reassure them that he would 'always be' Prince of Wales. It was an odd statement. Had the prince ever had a son, he would obviously have had to hand over the title; but perhaps, even then, he had a premonition that this would not happen. It would be many years before his great-nephew took the baton from him, and by then David was firmly ensconced in a place of exile near Paris.

All the new king could have meant when he talked about remaining Prince of Wales was that, there being officially no prince to represent them at that moment, the people of Wales could rely on him for support. When he arrived in Wales to visit the 'distressed areas' in the autumn of that year, great expectations accompanied him. He did not disappoint. His famous statement, that 'something must be done', has never been forgotten, and this fellow-feeling for the unemployed had much to do with memories of his war service. The working classes in Britain still had an inflated idea of the extent of their sovereign's power. When he said, 'Something must be done', they believed that something really *would* be done. Perhaps, at the time, the king thought so too; if so, he was soon to be disillusioned.

Since 1928, the Prince of Wales had spent much of his time at his bachelor pad, Fort Belvedere, a country retreat that gave him a degree of freedom today's royals would be lucky to enjoy. It was from Fort Belvedere that he made the announcement that shocked the nation, in December 1936. The king had been forced to make a choice between his kingdom and the woman he wanted to marry. He had chosen Wallis Simpson.

Opinions on Mrs Simpson scarcely vary. Few people seem really to have liked or admired her. Officials were unanimous in thinking her thick-skinned and ambitious, manipulative and concerned mostly with her own welfare; but then, it suited them to see her that way. It is said that she deliberately 'fed' information to the American press to ensure that her existence and Edward's devotion to her did not remain secret. Her political opinions were also suspect. It was rumoured that she had close links with the Germans and believed in dictatorship.

It has also been said that the new king tried to bargain with the prime minister, Stanley Baldwin, to get what he wanted, using abdication as a threat to persuade the government to agree to a morganatic marriage. His chosen wife was at an age (forty) when she was not likely to produce children, so he was bound to be succeeded eventually by his younger brother. It was not a problem for the king to strike his own children out of the line of succession. He did not, however, rush to give up the kingship. It would be nice to think that Edward VIII wanted to stay on because he had plans to improve things for the people of Wales, so badly affected by unemployment and economic depression. It is more likely that he had already begun to see that his hands would always be tied by political expediency.

The king had gone so far as to ask the influential newspaper tycoon Lord Beaverbrook to suppress the news of Mrs Simpson's divorce case, in October 1936. The British public had been kept out of the loop so far by the self-censorship of the UK press, and the leaks from across the Atlantic had been prevented from circulating by the expedient of physically cutting them out of American magazines sold in the UK. Cartoonist David Low, when visiting the USA, told an interviewer that 'when the King does decide to marry Mrs Simpson it will be popularly approved, not only romantically but politically'. Low was tired of being prevented from seeing his contributions on the subject in print. 'England', he said, 'wants a queen.'

No doubt many of the king's ordinary subjects would have agreed with the principle of allowing the sovereign to make his own choice, but the government did not. Beaverbrook's political allegiance was such that the prime minister, Baldwin, was portrayed as the villain of the piece, but the devious intentions of the editors were transparent. Churchill, who was more sympathetic to the king's wishes than Baldwin, advised him to play for time. In the end, however, it was 'the Establishment' who put paid to Edward VIII's hopes of having his cake and eating it. Bishops were already queueing up to express concern over the prospect of a divorcee becoming the wife of the head of the Church of England. Finally, the king surprised everyone by his readiness to be ousted. The truth is that he was temperamentally unsuited to the role of a constitutional monarch, and he knew it.

After his abdication, another title had to be found for the king. The situation had not arisen since the forced abdication of King James II of England and VII of Scotland, two hundred and fifty years earlier. The dukedom of Windsor was created for David's benefit, and he was known by that title until his death, nearly thirty-six years later. Although apparently reluctant to leave the throne, and continuing to hanker after an alternative

KING GEORGE AND THE PRINCE OF WALES AT THE FRONT

King George V encourages troops at the Western Front, while his son the Prince of Wales already looks bored.

role that would give him a purpose in the eyes of his former subjects, he was refused any opening in public life. We have learned, since his death, of his fascist sympathies, and it has been suggested that he was prepared to collaborate with the Nazis. Perhaps we should not be so surprised at this. 'National socialism' had many working-class supporters until its excesses became generally apparent.

Had she wanted only the position royalty gave her, Wallis Simpson had time to change her mind; the couple did not marry until June 1937. For Wallis to have dropped the king after he had given up the throne for her, however, would have taken more than average courage. The Duke and Duchess of Windsor remained married until his death in 1972. The assumption that the marriage was a happy one has never been seriously challenged. The duchess lived out the last fourteen years of her life as a recluse, her existence virtually ignored by the British royal family. She was never allowed the style of Her Royal Highness. When she died in 1986, her remains were brought to the UK without ceremony, and laid beside those of her husband in the royal mausoleum at Windsor.

The Present Day

Between Edward VIII and the present Prince of Wales, there was a gap of sixteen years during which the heir to the throne was female. Possible titles for Princess Elizabeth, the elder daughter of George VI, were discussed, but there was no useful precedent, though the title of 'Prince of Wales' had sometimes been applied to the daughters of Henry VIII in an honorary context. Neither Queen Anne nor Queen Victoria had been the reigning monarch's eldest child, and Mary II, besides being already married to William of Orange, had quickly been superseded by a younger brother, so the question had not arisen for any of them. There is still no precedent for a title for a king's eldest daughter, who by definition cannot be the heir apparent unless the laws of succession are changed (which will probably happen at some future date if the monarchy survives that long). 'Princess Royal' has been used only for princesses who were *not* first in line for the throne.

It was not until 1958, six years after her accession to the throne, that Elizabeth II confirmed her son, Charles, as Prince of Wales. She had chosen to save the announcement for a special occasion, and the occasion deemed suitable was the closing ceremony of the Commonwealth Games in Cardiff. The queen chose, also, to wait until Charles was a man before publicly investing him with the title.

When Charles was born, in November 1948, his mother was not yet queen. Most people have seen photographs of her coronation in 1953, when the four-year-old boy, with his toddler sister Anne, waved to the crowds from the balcony of Buckingham Palace. Charles was nearly twelve by the time he had a younger brother, and consequently had time to get used to the idea of

HRH The Prince of Wales uses his charm on Susan Cox, chairman of the Cowbridge Charter Trust, on a St David's Day visit to the town. Photo © Mike Baker.

being the alpha male in the family as well as the heir apparent. Interviewed shortly before the investiture, he looked back on his childhood, saying: 'I think it's something that dawns on you with the most ghastly, inexorable sense. I didn't suddenly wake up in my pram one day and say "Yippee," you know.'

Prince Philip, a man's man if ever there was one, was determined that his son would have the masculinity demanded of the heir to the throne. In the absence of a clear official role for the consort, the next best thing for Philip was to be instrumental in moulding the character of the future king. It is popularly believed that Charles rebelled against this upbringing, hated his time at Gordonstoun (his father's old school) and has never been close to Philip. Fifty years on, he still comes across as a gentler person, his strong opinions always constrained by an awareness of the need for diplomacy. This makes his occasional outbursts all the more effective.

On 1 July 1969, a few months before he turned twenty-one, Charles was invested at Caernarfon Castle, like his predecessor, Edward VIII. The ceremony, which must have appeared so formal and ancient to those watching, was no more traditional than the eisteddfod trappings dreamed up by Iolo Morganwg. It was Lloyd George's creation of 1911 that was really being revived. Overseen by the queen's brother-in-law, the Earl of Snowdon, the ceremony was attended by 4,000 invited guests and watched on television by an audience estimated at 500 million. The souvenirs and celebrations marking the occasion were such that, when Neil Armstrong stepped onto the surface of the moon later in the same month, some joked that this was yet another special event in honour of the investiture.

Like most of those who went before him, Charles was crowned with a coronet (a modernistic design that is now on display in the National Museum of Wales), and given a sword, a gold ring and a gold rod. He recited a set of archaic vows pledging his allegiance to his mother, and afterwards gave a speech in both English and Welsh. So conventional and clichéd were its words that one need hardly doubt he had a leading role in writing them. 'Wales needs to look forward without forsaking the traditions and essential aspects of her past. The past can be just as much a stimulus to the future as anything else.' Here is a statement designed to offend no one.

Charles was responding to a 'loyal address' by Sir Ben Bowen Thomas, president of the University College of Wales, in which Sir Ben expressed confidence that the newly invested prince would become a defender of the principality's traditions and language as well as assisting in the resolution of its problems. It was almost as if he believed that the prince had some political power.

The nationalist backlash was potentially violent. Using the symbol of the Snowdonian eagle as their flag, the six convicted members of the 'Free Wales Army' led a small extremist group that managed to plant no less than thirteen bombs in the period leading up to the investiture ceremony, but these were rather feeble efforts. The only casualties were two maverick bomb-makers, killed by their own device on their way to blow up a bridge. Perhaps more effective were the peaceful protests, such as the song 'Carlo', written and performed by the anti-establishment folk singer Dafydd Iwan (who later became president of Plaid Cymru). Extreme reactions, either for or against the investiture of an English prince, were infectious.

Charles had spent three months at the University College of Wales in Aberystwyth, ostensibly for a crash course in Welsh, but also perhaps with the intention of mixing with his future 'subjects' in order to get a feel for what was expected of him. Some students protested outside his hall of residence, whilst those inside launched a counter-attack. The chairman of the student union said he sensed 'a genuine feeling of interest by the Prince in learning as much as he can about the people and the country whose name he'll bear'. Charles's supporters were inspired by national feeling as much as their opponents were, but in a different way. The investiture duly went ahead, and the protests failed to mar the day. Charles took his place as the twenty-first 'official' Prince of Wales.

It is a title he has carried honourably in terms of his duty to the principality, and it has given him an identity and a recognizable role he might not otherwise have had. It is one thing to be the heir to a throne, but it is surely more meaningful to be specifically linked with a geographical region. The prince, of course, also has strong links with Cornwall, of which he has been Duke from birth. The Duchy brings with it enormous estates, estimated at 57,091 hectares, only 7,664 of which are in Cornwall. Like his ancestor, the Black Prince, Charles may sometimes face a conflict of territorial interests, though he receives no revenues from the principality.

Yet Charles Windsor is seen by many as a very imperfect prince. In his youth, he appeared the ideal heir, never caught out in an indiscretion. (Only much later did the public learn how his great-uncle, Earl Mountbatten, had encouraged him to experiment with the opposite sex and assisted him in keeping these activities a secret.) Some may have felt Charles was too old for his years; even as a teenager, he never seemed to be interested in the pursuits typical of that age group. He simply could not win. He seemed, briefly, to have redeemed himself when he married, at the age of thirty-two, the chaste English rose Lady Diana Spencer, though many were concerned about the age difference of twelve years between them. When Diana proceeded to give birth to two bouncing baby boys, the couple became extremely popular, and Charles was seen as settling down at last to family life and recognizing his responsibilities. At one point, the South Wales Police had to suggest to the couple that they should cut down on their visits to Wales because of the enormous cost of the additional security required. This was mostly to hold back admirers, not protesters.

Later, when it was learnt that Charles had in fact had a love affair with Camilla Parker-Bowles both before and after their respective marriages, public sympathy fell off. He was perceived very much as the guilty party in the long-running divorce scandal, and even since Diana's death he has had a lot of ground to make up. All the revelations about Diana's personal life have done little to help the prince regain his popularity. What most people find difficult to understand is why he did not marry Camilla when he had the opportunity. There were many years of bachelorhood when everyone was on the lookout for a suitable wife for him; perhaps the truth is that the prince himself considered Camilla Shand unsuitable at the time. Somehow the fact that Charles is godfather to Camilla's son, Tom Parker-Bowles, seems even more shocking to the public than the parallel situation that existed when the Black Prince married Joan of Kent.

Yet Charles, like so many of his less savoury predecessors, charms those who meet him. He is a professional royal, but tempers his regal duties with a sympathy for the aspirations of ordinary people, conveying an image his late princess assisted him in creating. In fairness, he has always had a social conscience. The Prince's Trust, set up in 1976 (long before Charles had any children of his own) as a charity for young people, is known throughout the UK. Charles, despite having two younger brothers, was indisputably 'the prince' until the birth of his first son.

We live in an age where the Prince of Wales considers it his duty not only to assume certain responsibilities towards Wales (in his honorary capacity as Prince of Wales) and towards the UK and Commonwealth (in his more tangible role as heir to the throne), but to let everyone know about it. Hence his website, which contains more words than are in this book, and two 'brochures' which he publishes, describing the work he has been doing. The Prince's Trust is a high-profile charity, but its work tends to be regarded, at least by those who have not benefited from it, as a rich man's philanthropy, perhaps because of the self-help philosophy that governs its running. It is in fact a sophisticated cooperative effort, drawing in donations from organizations which might otherwise be reluctant to involve themselves in an operation that aims to help young offenders as well as those attempting to start up in business. At the thirtieth anniversary of the Trust's foundation, one of the success stories put forward was that of Mark Johnson, a former heroin addict turned company director. Johnson's example is typical.

Prince Charles had begun his progress down the philanthropic road before he married Diana Spencer in 1981. Diana had a profound influence both on the public image of the royal family and on their actual roles within the country and Commonwealth, but she cannot be credited with forcing the prince to recognize his responsibilities; he was already well aware of them. What he found difficult, before, during and after his marriage, was to form a personal relationship with his people. It is surely no coincidence that the first Prince's Trust Rock Gala was staged two years *after* the royal wedding. With the assistance of experts, Charles has become a consummate self-publicist, but he still lacks the common touch. It remains to be seen whether his elder son will succeed in breaking the mould.

Charles has faced the same quandary as his ancestor Edward VII: how to create for himself a recognizable role which can at best only be semi-official. His title of Duke of Cornwall helps; he owns so much property that he can afford to experiment, and, as he is a landowner, his interests tend towards agriculture and outdoor pursuits. It is in the area of conservation and the environment that the prince's influence has been most strongly noticed by the general public.

In 1984, speaking to the Royal Institute of British Architects about the proposed extension to the National Gallery in Trafalgar Square, he made the memorable remark that it resembled 'a monstrous carbuncle on the face of a much-loved and elegant friend'. In the same speech, he referred back to the architectural activities of his ancestor, Prince Albert, as though anxious to remind his audience of the historical precedent for royalty meddling in such matters. Concerned about appearing reactionary, he took a more conciliatory approach to the erection of a glass pyramid outside the main entrance to the Louvre in 1989, praising the design by modernist architect I. M. Pei. In 1992, Charles started up his own organization, the Prince of Wales's Institute for Architecture, remarking in his inauguration speech that he often woke up 'sweating' in the middle of the night, wondering if he had been too ambitious.

The architecture of Wales has not entirely escaped his notice. Another of his brainchildren, the Foundation for the Built Environment, has taken on the task of developing an 'urban village' at the former oil refinery site of Llandarcy in south Wales. On the launch of the foundation in 1998, he wrote an article for *The Spectator* entitled 'Why I'm modern but not a modernist', in which he summarizes his motives and beliefs. If the article had appeared in a less highbrow publication, it might have done more to improve his overall image.

In 2003, an editorial in *The Observer* called Charles 'this meddlesome prince' and made the following comments:

> Dismissing the prince as irrelevant is as mistaken as it is tempting. His nanophobia, a prejudice dismissed as ludicrous by laureates, or anyone with a physics A-level, is only the latest in a Pooterish list. GM crops, carbuncular architecture, greedy supermarkets,

human rights and the fate of oppressed farmers, who fare worse
than 'ethnic minorities and gays', have equally enraged him.

What the writer seems to have overlooked is that these are
views shared by the majority of the public, and to call the
prince 'a regressive xenophobe' is simply to prove oneself out
of touch with public opinion. So perhaps the prince's subjects
would think him not so bad if they could only get to know
him better.

Indeed, they did think better of him during the late 1980s
and early 1990s, as demonstrated by the 1993 television drama
serial, *To Play the King*, in which a barely disguised royal
character grapples with corrupt politicians and unsuccessfully
attempts to assert his constitutional role. This was shortly after
the Prince of Wales had separated from his first wife, and the
sordid 'Camillagate' tapes (in which Camilla is heard to say, in
an apparent reference to the Duchess of Westminster, 'those
sort of people do feel very strongly about you') were not
popularly believed to be genuine.

Following his divorce, in response to criticism that he was
spending too little time in Wales, Charles began holding honours
ceremonies within the principality, to save Welsh recipients
from having to travel to London. Most importantly, he was in
Cardiff in 1999 for the opening of the Welsh Assembly.
Although he could hardly have stayed away from such an
occasion, he chose to underline the significance of his presence
by making a speech in Welsh. 'Wales has its own identity and
voice,' he said, in a style reminiscent of his investiture speech.
'The assembly is part of its evolution into a distinct and vibrant
country, playing an important role in the UK and on the world
stage.'

Anyone who takes a brief look back over the centuries, as
this book has attempted to do, will recognize how very little
regard Charles's predecessors have shown for their nominal
principality. Few of them visited at all, let alone regularly. As a
boy and a young man, Charles spent a good deal of time in
Wales, notably his term in residence at Aberystwyth, and his
visits were mostly well received, but in recent years his relationship with the principality has cooled somewhat. Nationalism
in the twenty-first century is as strong as it has been at any

time since Edward I's conquest. Nevertheless, there are many who regard our present prince as a figurehead and more, a likely ambassador for Wales and our true representative in government. The principality gives him a solid base from which to rebuild his popularity within the UK as a whole. It remains to be seen whether his choice of second wife will be a hindrance or a help in that process.

In a private conversation during 2005, a former employee of the prince's told me that he believes Charles 'will make a very good king'. When I expressed doubt as to whether Charles actually *wanted* to become king, he seemed barely to have considered this possibility, and was adamant that the Prince of Wales will one day rule. Notwithstanding this personal view from someone who knows the prince very well, many have speculated on the possibility of his being 'passed over' for the throne. Being passed over is not a constitutional possibility, but it *is* possible for any British monarch to decide to abdicate after a very short tenure; there is one very good precedent for this. The prince, on the other hand, has recently denied rumours that he intends to rule as King George VII, not King Charles III. Such a discussion would be academic if he intends not to rule at all.

Charles is now in a precarious position as far as his path to the throne is concerned. Past kings and princes have been able to live openly with mistresses and, although public opinion may have been against them, they had the power to ignore the views of others and do as they wished. Increasingly, since Parliament began to take both power and the right to an income out of the hands of the monarchy, this kind of conduct has become unacceptable. Wynford Vaughan-Thomas, writing about the birth of Prince William (a recent event when his study of the Princes of Wales was published) noted that 'the future of the monarchy may quite literally be in the hands of the child'. He made this prediction without any intimation of the scandals that would shortly beset the royal family.

Whereas some of Charles's predecessors, such as Henry V and Edward VII, redeemed their misspent youth when they became kings instead of princes, others, like the Black Prince, found equal fame as Prince of Wales. One must ask this: would it be such a terrible thing if Charles never became king? Might it not be considered that he has done enough for the country (the UK, that is) in his role as Prince of Wales? There has been speculation that the statement of intent made at the time of his wedding to the Duchess of Cornwall, namely that she would take the title of Princess Consort when her husband ascends the throne, is merely 'testing the water' and that she will in fact be styled queen. However, the opposite could easily be true. Charles may be content to allow his wife never to be called queen, simply because he himself does not plan to be called king. Time alone will tell.

Select Bibilography

Abse, Joan (ed.), *Letters from Wales* (Poetry Wales Press, 2000).

Ashdown, Dulcie M., *Princess of Wales* (John Murray, 1979).

Bowle, John, *Charles the First* (Weidenfeld & Nicolson, 1975).

Cannon, John and Griffiths, Ralph (eds), *Oxford Illustrated History of the British Monarchy*, revised edn (Oxford University Press, 2000).

Davies, R. R., *Wales: The Age Of Conquest, 1063–1415* (Oxford University Press, 1987).

——, *The Revolt of Owain Glyn Dŵr* (Oxford University Press, 1995).

Falkus, Christopher, *The Life and Times of Charles II* (Weidenfeld & Nicolson, 1972).

Fisher, Deborah, *Princesses of Wales* (University of Wales Press, 2005).

Hibbert, Christopher, *George IV: Prince of Wales* (Longman, 1972).

Hicks, Michael, *Edward V: The Prince in the Tower* (Tempus, 2003).

Jones, Francis, *The Princes and Principality of Wales* (University of Wales Press, 1969).

Palmer, Alan, *Princes of Wales* (Weidenfeld & Nicolson, 1979).

Pine, L. G., *Princes of Wales* (Herbert Jenkins, 1959).

Sadler, Mary, *Edward II* (Rubicon Press, 1997).

Strong, Roy, *Henry, Prince of Wales and England's Lost Renaissance* (Pimlico, 2000).

Townsend, W. and L., *The Biography of HRH the Prince of Wales* (Albert E. Marriott & Son, 1929).

Turvey, Roger, *The Welsh Princes 1063–1283* (Longman, 2002).

Vaughan-Thomas, Wynford, *The Princes of Wales* (Kaye & Ward, 1982).

Index